DEEDS
★ NOT ★
WORDS

Celebrating 100 Years of Women's Suffrage

Sandra Sider & Pamela Weeks

4880 Lower Valley Road • Atglen, PA 19310

Designed by Ashley Millhouse
Cover design by Ashley Millhouse
Type set in GriffosFont/Berthold Baskerville

ISBN: 978-0-7643-5917-0
Printed in China

Published by Schiffer Publishing, Ltd.
4880 Lower Valley Road
Atglen, PA 19310
Phone: (610) 593-1777; Fax: (610) 593-2002
E-mail: Info@schifferbooks.com
Web: www.schifferbooks.com

For our complete selection of fine books on this and related subjects, please visit our website at www.schifferbooks.com. You may also write for a free catalog.

Schiffer Publishing's titles are available at special discounts for bulk purchases for sales promotions or premiums. Special editions, including personalized covers, corporate imprints, and excerpts, can be created in large quantities for special needs. For more information, contact the publisher.

We are always looking for people to write books on new and related subjects. If you have an idea for a book, please contact us at proposals@schifferbooks.com.

Front cover images:
Sandy Curran | *Honor Her* (2019), 50 × 31 in.
Adrienne Yorinks | *Resistance to Tyranny Is Obedience to God* (1995), 79 × 71 in. | *Photo by Craig Dietrich*
Hope Wilmarth | *Tour de Force* (2018, text of 19th Amendment), 45 × 34 in. | *Photo by Rick Wells*
Alice Beasley | *She Refused to Walk Behind* (2019, Ida Wells), 35.25 × 40 in. | *Photo by Sibila Savage Photography*

Back cover image:
Hollis Chatelain | *Federation Gertie*

OTHER SCHIFFER BOOKS BY THE AUTHORS:

Exploring Your Artistic Voice in Contemporary Quilt Art,
Sandra Sider, ISBN 9780764358876

Art Quilts Unfolding: 50 Years of Innovation,
Sandra Sider , editor, Nancy Bavor, Lisa Ellis, Martha Sielman,
SAQA (Studio Art Quilt Associates, Inc.), ISBN 9780764356261
Civil War Quilts, 2nd Edition, Pamela Weeks and Don Beld, ISBN
978-0-7643-5888-3

OTHER SCHIFFER BOOKS ON RELATED SUBJECTS:

HERstory Quilts: A Celebration of Strong Women,
Susanne Miller Jones, ISBN 9780764354601

And Still We Rise: Race, Culture and Visual Conversations,
Carolyn L. Mazloomi, ISBN 9780764349287

Visioning Human Rights in the New Millennium: Quilting the World's Conscience,
Carolyn L. Mazloomi, ISBN 9780764357404

Artists clockwise from top left: Jill Kerttula, Teresa Barkley, Pixeladies, and Therese May

Contents

Introduction

THE CONCEPT FOR THIS EXHIBITION ORIGINATED WITH JUDY SCHWENDER, former curator at the National Quilt Museum, who organized dozens of exhibitions during her years of service. Early in 2017, she invited the two of us to collaborate on creating a touring exhibition to commemorate the one hundredth anniversary of the Nineteenth Amendment to the US Constitution:

SECTION 1.

The right of the citizens of the United States to vote shall not be denied or abridged by the United States or by any State on account of sex.

SECTION 2.

Congress shall have power to enforce this article by appropriate legislation.

After considering a juried exhibition, we decided instead to invite award-winning artists from across the United States, each to make a quilt celebrating women's suffrage. We were thrilled with the number of artists who accepted our invitation! The artists chose their own topics, without any censorship on our part; we asked only that no two artists honor the same suffragist. Our *Deeds not Words* exhibition presents twenty-eight art quilts by twenty-nine artists (the Pixeladies being a collaborative duo). We included two essays, one on the quilts and the other on women's suffrage—an even more complicated subject than you might think. It was important to us that we include male artists in the exhibition, to recognize the support of many men concerning women's suffrage, and to feature several African-American artists and subjects. Although the Nineteenth Amendment made a huge stride forward for women's rights, in many voting situations that right extended only to white women because of prejudicial practices.

Long before the quilts were completed, we were gratified to be able to book the exhibition's entire tour, from 2020 until 2022. We had the very good fortune of having Luana Rubin at eQuilter.com enthusiastically in favor of the exhibition, and having eQuilter as our exclusive sponsor is something for which we are immensely grateful. Additional recognition is due Karey Bresenhan and Nancy O'Bryant Puentes, who generously offered the resources of the Texas Quilt Museum to expedite aspects of managing and shipping the show, and we thank them both.

Sandra Sider, Curator, Texas Quilt Museum
Pamela Weeks, Curator, New England Quilt Museum

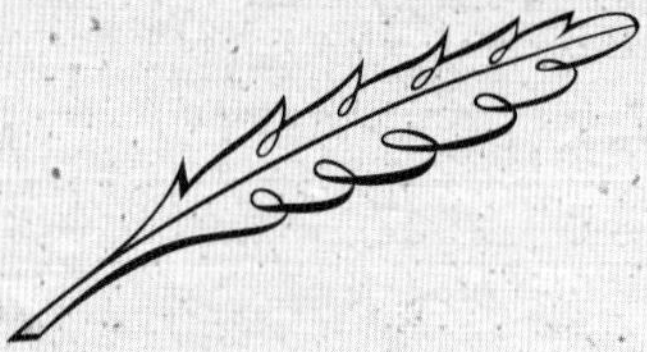

A Brief History
of the Struggle

Pamela Weeks

THE CAMPAIGN TO GAIN THE VOTE FOR WOMEN WAS NOT A straightforward, single-line battle with a few key players that lasted for part of the nineteenth century and into the twentieth, as I was taught in school. Rather, for more than eighty years, it was a splintered, multiorganizational, highly nuanced social, political, and racial struggle with a multitude of leaders, black and white. It encompassed not just the goal to win the vote for women for the early organizers, but also to gain complete equality with men in all aspects of property ownership, educational and professional opportunities, work wages, and citizens' rights. The campaign in the United States was interrupted by three wars, splintered by differing viewpoints on what rights should be fought for, and further divided by the racism of some of its leaders.

During the American Revolution, in anticipation of the work of the Second Constitutional Convention, which would write the Declaration of Independence and the United States Constitution, Abigail Adams in 1776 wrote to her husband, John:

> *I long to hear that you have declared an independency—and by the way in the new Code of Laws which I suppose it will be necessary for you to make I desire you would Remember the Ladies, and be more generous and favourable to them than your ancestors. Do not put such unlimited power into the hands of the Husbands. Remember all Men would be tyrants if they could. If perticuliar care and attention is not paid to the Ladies we are determined to foment a Rebelion, and will not hold ourselves bound by any Laws in which we have no voice, or Representation.*

The first few decades of the nineteenth century saw the Second Great Awakening, a period when many people became deeply religious in thought and, in action, worked for social change. Abolishing slavery, curtailing the consumption of alcohol, improving education for all classes of citizens, and securing equal rights for women headed the list of social reforms for which thousands advocated. Some prominent leaders of the women's rights movements were Quakers, whose religious doctrine had always considered women equal to men. This period saw a general shift from women being working partners with their husbands in their businesses or on farms, to moving to the towns and cities, where they were ensconced in the "sphere of domesticity." Husbands left the home to work in the professions, and most women stayed to manage the household and raise children.

The relative safety within this sphere often served as an obstacle that kept some women from joining the fight for equal rights. Those women didn't want change, and they formed organizations to work against suffrage and equal rights. However, many women did do reform work beyond temperance or the abolition of slavery, and they began to demand equal rights for women.

The Industrial Revolution, which began with the mechanization of the production of cloth and helped create the separate spheres for men and women, also provided the first real opportunity for women to work outside the home and earn a wage. Many young women left their farms and moved to the quickly growing factory cities in the Northeast, and some of them became activists, first striking for equal pay in Dover, New Hampshire, in 1828. The Woman's Rights Convention was organized by Elizabeth Cady Stanton and Lucretia Mott (a Quaker leader already prominent in the antislavery movement) in 1848 in Seneca Falls, New York. Its outcome was the Declaration of Sentiments, modeled after the Declaration of Independence. It stated in part: "We hold these truths to be self-evident: that all men and women are created equal." The declaration included a list of rights that all citizens should share, including suffrage; the right for women to hold property in their own names; the right to a divorce and to retain custody of their children; and the right to attend universities and pursue careers in medicine or law. Frederick Douglass and other prominent abolitionists spoke, and a strong alliance with the abolitionist movement continued.

During the Civil War, most activity concerning women's rights ceased as the country turned to support the war effort on all fronts. A year after the end of the war, in 1866, leaders of the women's rights movement convened another Woman's Rights Convention and formed the American Equal Rights Association (AERA), with the purpose of securing the vote for all citizens, regardless of race or sex. One of the speakers was Frances Ellen Watkins Harper, an African-American poet and novelist well known for her intellect and oration, who demanded that the women's rights movement

QUILT, EMMA CIVEY STAHL, ILLINOIS
Cotton, 70 × 69.5 in.
Courtesy of the Metropolitan Museum of Art, New York, 2011.538
This is the only known quilt with images of a woman involved in the women's rights movement. In the circular vignettes, she is shown exiting home, leaving family behind, with a woman's rights banner over her shoulder, and lecturing. Is the maker of the quilt in favor of women's rights, or showing the consequences of involvement in the campaign?

advocate for equal rights and suffrage for all. She and many other women of color were later written out of the history of the movement by Elizabeth Cady Stanton and Susan B. Anthony.

In 1869 a major rift opened within the AERA when a faction led by Stanton and Anthony was angered by the passage of the Fourteenth Amendment, which gave citizenship to former slaves but defined voters as male only. This faction refused to support the proposed Fifteenth Amendment, granting voting rights to black American males, ignoring female suffrage completely. Instead, they founded the National Woman Suffrage Association (NWSA), working to achieve the vote and other women's rights through a constitutional amendment. Stanton in particular was derided by prominent leaders for her racist characterization of black men.

Conservative activists Lucy Stone, Julia Ward Howe, and others formed the American Woman Suffrage Association (AWSA) to work for women's suffrage through amending individual state constitutions. For twenty years the organizations worked on parallel tracks, reuniting in 1890 for the final push toward a constitutional amendment. Many other women entered the fight. Victoria Woodhull ran for US president in 1872 and was jailed. Her advocacy for free love, open marriage, and women's rights brought notoriety and unwelcome scandal. A group of influential New York society women joined the cause in the early twentieth century and are given credit by many for pushing the issue to its successful conclusion through their skillful use of the press.

In 1920, with the ratification of the Nineteenth Amendment, American women finally achieved the right to vote. One hundred forty-four years after Abigail Adams implored her husband to "remember the ladies," women were guaranteed only the right to vote–the struggle for equality continues.

Pam Weeks's love for quilts began at the time of the United States bicentennial in 1976. With many other women at the time of this great quilting revival, she took her first quilting class. Weeks made traditional and then art quilts, but in 1991 she began an exploration of quilt history, women's history, and textile history that continues today. Her work on signature quilts and potholder quilts is found in the American Quilt Study Group's peer-reviewed journal Uncoverings, *and in 2011 she published* Civil War Quilts *with coauthor Don Beld. She is the Binney Family Curator at the New England Quilt Museum in Lowell, Massachusetts.*

QUILT BLOCK, MAKER UNKNOWN

Cotton, 15 × 15 in.

Durham Historic Association, Durham, New Hampshire | *Photograph by Pamela Weeks*

This redwork square (embroidered with red thread), perhaps made for a quilt project, was found in the collection of the Durham Historic Association, with no provenance indicated. The women, dressed in wooden shoes and a cap similar to costumes worn in the Netherlands, hold flags embroidered with "Equal Rights" and "Votes for Women." Such examples of suffragist needlework are extremely rare.

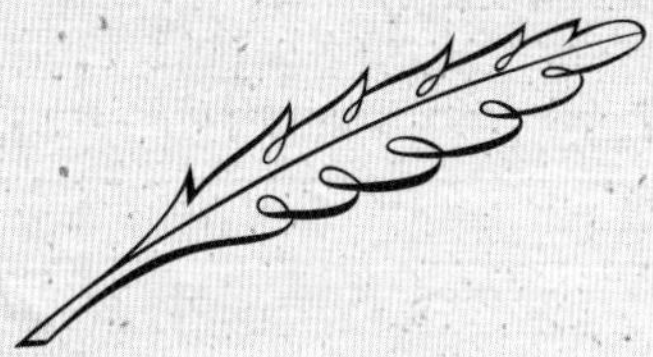

"Deeds not Words": Celebrating 100 Years of Women's Suffrage

by Sandra Sider

THIS EXHIBITION OF STUDIO ART QUILTS WAS CREATED WITH THE understanding that many of the suffragists celebrated here would find the concept of commemorating women's suffrage in the United States via needlework to be somewhat ironic. Some of the leaders in the movement shunned their domestic duties–which, of course, usually were being done by hired women and girls–to follow a higher calling. They were ridiculed in cartoons at the time. While fashionable attire was deemed important to present an acceptable public image, we can assume that the suffragists were not taking the time to stitch those silk dresses themselves, even though they often produced their own flags, banners, rosettes, and sashes.

EMMELINE PANKHURST, THE FAMOUSLY MILITANT BRITISH SUFFRAGIST, in 1903 coined the motto "Deeds not Words" for the newly formed Women's Social and Political Union. She felt the need for violent action after half a century of effort had not changed the discrimination against franchising women. History has proven that well-crafted rhetoric is the impetus for deeds, which are often the final steps needed for radical change. Many of the quilts in this exhibition remind us all of the power and necessity of our First Amendment.

By quoting their words and reproducing their portraits, approximately half of the *Deeds not Words* quilts honor a specific suffragist, some more famous than others and some quite controversial, with the portraits ranging from actual photographic reproductions to Sojourner Truth interpreted by Therese May as a dynamic twenty-first-century figure. The suffragists were true revolutionaries, occasionally sacrificing their reputations and freedom. They were the original "nasty" women, with the *New York Times* in 1906 derisively commenting, "Suffragette (Strix Flagitans): A woman who ought to have more sense." That Latin phrase, coined by a male journalist, means "demanding screecher." Because "suffragette" was meant to be a demeaning term at the time, Pamela Weeks and I are using the term "suffragist" throughout this book.

Several of our artists chose to celebrate a suffragist whose name they remembered from history lessons, while others felt a more personal relationship with their subjects. Arturo Alonzo Sandoval, for example, was inspired by a friend who is the daughter of an African-American suffragist; Martha Wolfe studied Sara Bard Field, who road-tripped from San Francisco to Washington, DC, collecting signatures for women's suffrage; North Carolina artist Hollis Chatelain honors Gertrude Weil; Chicago artist Laura Wasilowski celebrates Jane Addams; Alice Beasley's quilt depicts the courageous Ida B. Wells; Robin Schwalb was drawn to Amelia Bloomer and her fashion radicalism; and, Jill Kerttula's multipart quilt reminds us that Belva Lockwood in 1884 ran for president, even though she herself was not permitted to vote.

Other artists focused on group activities and issues involving women's rights, such as Jayne Gaskins's piece about the road to legislation, with a nod to #MeToo, and suffragist demonstrations depicted by Patricia Kennedy-Zafred. The two-part quilt by Caryl Bryer Fallert-Gentry includes a fabric panel that can be lifted to reveal a list of notable "first ladies" and their achievements, of which my personal favorite is Sally Ride, the first American woman in outer space and a role model to girls everywhere. Teresa Barkley references suffragist activities during the Boston Tea Party centennial, an example of how suffragists were successfully publicizing their cause.

While the majority of quilts in *Deeds not Words* are mostly two-dimensional wall art, three works are more sculptural. Susan Lenz created a folding diptych for Lucy Stone, inspired by her image in daguerreotype and impressed by the fact that she refused to relinquish her surname upon marriage—for which she and her husband wrote their own vows. John Lefelhocz's mixed-media quilt with backlighting stands approximately 3 inches deep, with an interactive feature allowing viewers to change the lighting by the "deed" of moving around. Clara Foltz is interpreted by Maria Billings as a pillar of her community, and the entire quilt can be curved outward from the wall to create a semicolumnar form.

Except for Adrienne Yorinks, all the artists created original quilts specifically for this exhibition. Yorinks graciously allowed us to include her 1995 quilt *Resistance to Tyranny Is Obedience to God*, which was juried into the 1997 Quilt National exhibition. She made this quilt to celebrate the seventy-fifth anniversary of women's suffrage after visiting Women's Rights National Park in Seneca Falls, New York, the location of the first Woman's Rights Convention and the 1848 signing of the Declaration of Sentiments supporting women's suffrage. Yorinks reproduced that historic text in her photomontage quilt. Each quilt in *Deeds not Words* will reward you upon close inspection, with pictorial and textual messages occasionally embedded in the stitching.

Suffragist button, black on gold lustre, ⁷/₈ in., c. 1915.
Collection of Sandra Sider

Sandra Sider, a studio quilt artist since the 1980s, has led critique workshops for Studio Art Quilt Associates (SAQA) since 2005. She holds an MA in art history from the Institute of Fine Arts, New York University. Between 2010 and 2013, Sider served as president of SAQA, and today she is editor of SAQA's Art Quilt Quarterly as well as curator of the Texas Quilt Museum. She has written or edited more than a dozen books concerning contemporary quilt art. Her latest book, Exploring Your Artistic Voice, *is the inspirational culmination of her many years of critiquing and writing about the art quilt medium. www.sandrasider.com*

"The right of the citizens of the United States to vote shall not be denied or abridged by the United States or by any State on account of sex."

(19th Amendment)

The Quilts

Teresa Barkley

I DESIGNED THIS QUILT AS IF IT WERE A POSTAGE STAMP COMMEMORATING the centennial of women's suffrage in 2020. The design was inspired when I discovered that the women's suffrage organizations used the centennial of the Boston Tea Party in 1873 as an opportunity to demonstrate in Boston and New York City. Suffragists echoed our founding fathers with cries of "No taxation without representation." The famous cartoonist Thomas Nast drew an image of suffragists pouring tea into the harbor. In the years that followed, individual women and women's groups hosted tea parties to support the right for women to vote. *Tea Box to Ballot Box* depicts tea crates floating down a river from Boston, past New York City, Trenton, and Philadelphia, ultimately to arrive in Washington, DC, where they have been transformed into a ballot box. The quilt consists of five horizontal bands representing the states of Massachusetts, New York, New Jersey, and Pennsylvania. The bottom band represents Washington, DC. The fabrics suggest not only the flow of water and tea, but also the flow of ideas and the flow of time. The narrow bands of stars and stripes represent a "state line," as the tea crates move from state to state. Tablecloths are pieced together using patriotic prints, especially stars and stripes, representing individual states on the American flag. The suffragists' ultimate success was achieved by persevering state by state. On the night of December 16, 1773, colonists threw 342 chests of tea from three ships in Boston Harbor, in protest of a law that they considered unfair because they had no representation in the government. The suffragists considered this action a patriotic act, and they appealed to the public to consider their cause equally patriotic.

This artist's passion for working with fabric began at the age of five, when her mother taught her how to sew. Barkley received her formal education in textiles at the University of Delaware and the Fashion Institute of Technology. In 1980 she began her career as a patternmaker in New York, working for a variety of dress and sportswear manufacturers, including Perry Ellis and Shoshanna. Barkley's distinctive art quilts use recycled materials in combination with new materials. Her work can be found in several museum collections, including the Smithsonian, and has been illustrated in more than one hundred publications.

Alice Beasley

IN THE BUILDUP TO THE CELEBRATION OF THE CENTENNIAL OF THE Nineteenth Amendment, it is important to place the suffragist movement within the context of this nation's troubled history of racism. The truth is that, while fighting for the noble cause of women's right to vote, many suffragists, including such stars as Elizabeth Cady Stanton, nevertheless found themselves fully aligned with the racism of Jim Crow that gripped the nation following the Civil War. My quilt depicts one incident in this lesser-known battle within the suffragist movement, involving black civil rights activist and journalist Ida B. Wells. Wells was already a national figure and a journalist famous for her courageous antilynching campaigns when she traveled to Washington, DC, in 1913 to join the suffrage parade being organized by the leading suffrage association. Arriving with a delegation of members from Chicago, Wells was told by the head of the Illinois delegation that the national organization wanted "to keep the delegation entirely white." All black delegates, including Wells, were to walk at the end of the parade, behind the men, in a separate "colored" section. Wells refused. Instead of going to the back with other African Americans, Wells waited with spectators as the parade was underway, and stepped into the white Chicago delegation as they passed by. This was not Wells's first refusal to accept the place assigned to her by white society. In 1884 she sued a railroad line when they dragged her from the first-class ladies' car for refusing to ride in the smoking car—even though she had a first-class ticket. Seventy years before Rosa Parks, she won her case in the trial court only to have it reversed by the Tennessee Supreme Court.

I have been making portraits of people and objects since 1988. Fabric is my chosen medium of expression through which I incorporate the same light, shadow, and realistic perspective used by artists in other media. Rather than using paint, dyes, or other surface treatments, however, I rely instead on finding color, line, and texture in the print of commercial fabric and thread, or in fabrics that I print myself. www.alicebeasley.com

CLARA Shortridge FOLTZ

[Jul. 16, 1849 (Indiana)] Senator [?]

Ulkers, fought for your rights. [?] [?] [?] age 85.

1877: First public lecturer and an attorney [?]. [?] from [?] [?]

1878: Single mother of five, [?] and [?]

1878: First female lawyer admitted to the California State Bar

1879: FIRST [?] [?] [?] [?]

1880: FIRST female legislative counsel [?] [?]

1881: FIRST woman [?] prosecutor [?]

1893: FIRST to propose the creation of [?] [?]

1910: FIRST woman on the State Board of Omaha and Corrections [?]

[1930] 1911: FIRST female Deputy District [?] [?]

Photo by Visual Simplicity

Maria Billings

IT SEEMS TO ME THAT CLARA SHORTRIDGE FOLTZ AND I LIVED NEXT to each other for a large part of this year (2018). In June, Sandra Sider invited me to contribute an art quilt honoring Foltz (1849–1934) for this exhibition. Feeling very honored, I must also admit that I hadn't heard about Clara Foltz and neither had Sandra! One of Sandra's granddaughters, who resides in Los Angeles, researched this suffragist for an elementary school project and suggested her for this exhibition. Interesting months followed: researching about Foltz's life on the internet, in university libraries, and newspaper archives, reading her biography *Woman Lawyer* by Barbara Babcock, and then visualizing what had captivated me about her. I divided my summary of her life into two categories: characteristics and facts. Both are written on her elongated skirt in a columnar format, since she was a pillar of female achievement. Foltz often reminded her audiences, "Others fought for your rights. Use them." I think that this attitude is now more relevant than ever.

- 1878: First female lawyer admitted to the California State Bar

- 1879: First female clerk for the State Assembly's Judiciary Committee

- 1880: First female legislative council

- 1881: First female special prosecutor

- 1893: First to propose the creation of a "public defender"

- 1910: First woman on the State Board of Charities and Corrections

- 1910: First female deputy district attorney (age sixty-one)

- 1930: First woman to run for governor of California (age eighty-one)

Maria Billings is a bicultural artist (Europe, USA). In 1980, she earned a BA degree in textile and fiber art at the University of Cologne, Germany. Billings specializes in handmade textile images. Starting with either her own photography or a hand-painted background, she stitches the image to create more-tactile values, often with three-dimensional effects. Her inspiration stems from her respect for nature and people, as her artistic explorations lead to representational as well as abstract art. Billings has works in private and public collections around the world. www.MariaBillings.com

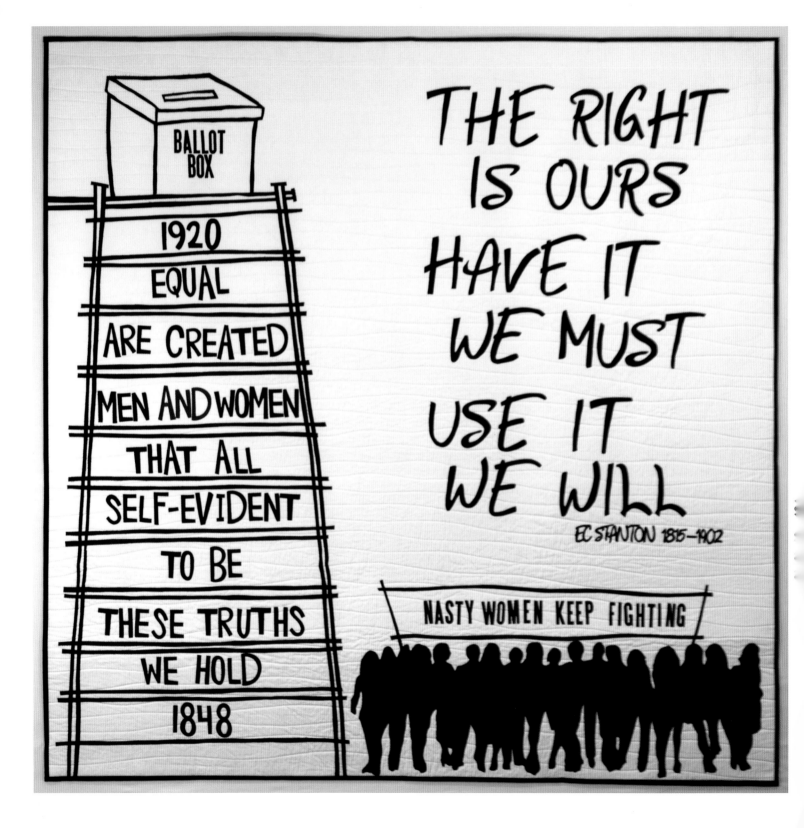

Sue Bleiweiss

ALTHOUGH SHE WAS ONE OF THE MOST PROMINENT FIGURES IN THE history of suffrage, Elizabeth Cady Stanton's name is not one that most associate with it. While doing my research on her, I came across a quote of hers: "The right is ours, have it we must, use it we will." This statement really spoke to me, and so I decided that it would be a key element on the quilt. I also wanted to include imagery that represented the long climb from the moment that Cady Stanton gave her speech at Seneca Falls in 1848 to the year that Congress finally adopted the Nineteenth Amendment, granting women the right to vote. I decided on incorporating a ladder that would include a quote from the Declaration of Sentiments, which she wrote. She cleverly expanded on the Declaration of Independence when she wrote the Declaration of Sentiments by adding the words "woman" or "women" throughout. This pivotal document called for social and legal changes to elevate women's place in society, and listed eighteen grievances, from the inability to control their wages and property and the difficulty in gaining custody in divorce, to the lack of a right to vote. It was a rallying cry for political, social, and economic equality for women, and it launched the beginning of the women's suffrage and equal rights movements in the United States. Cady Stanton was a formidable woman, steadfast in her belief that it was a woman's right to control her own circumstances; one for which she fought tirelessly.

Fiber artist Sue Bleiweiss creates vibrantly colorful and whimsical collages using her own hand-dyed cotton. She is the author of several books, a regular contributor to Quilting Arts Magazine, *and has made several television appearances, including* The Quilt Show with Alex Anderson and Ricky Tims, *and* Quilting Arts TV. *Her quilts have been exhibited internationally, and several are owned by private collections.* www.suebleiweiss.com

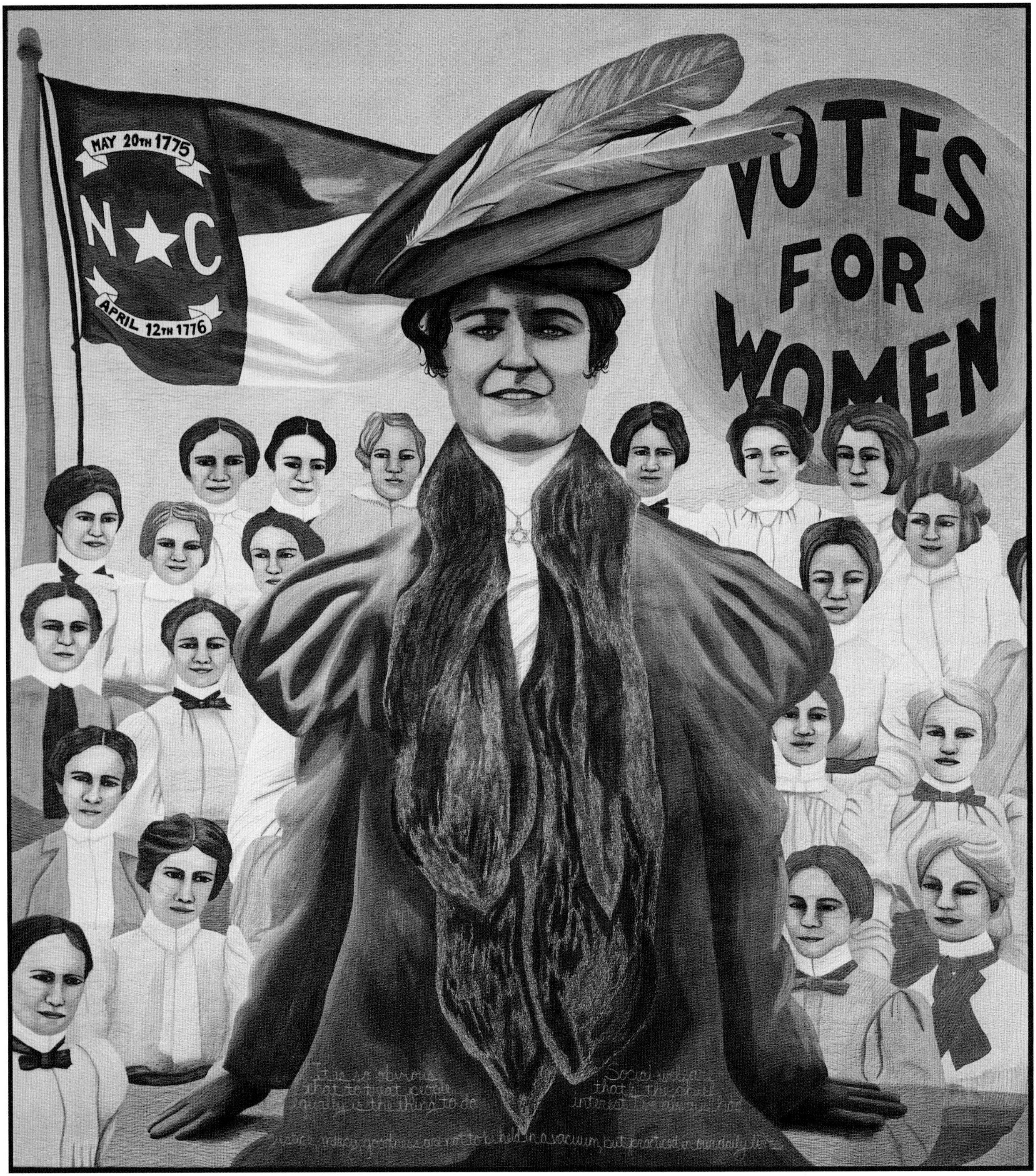

MAY 20TH 1775
N C
APRIL 12TH 1776
VOTES FOR WOMEN
It is so obvious
that to treat people
equally is the thing to do
Social welfare
that's the civil
interest I've always had

Hollis Chatelain

GERTRUDE WEIL WAS A MOVER AND SHAKER HER ENTIRE LIFE. UNAFRAID to voice her opinion, she followed in her mother's footsteps in fighting for social welfare at an early age. She continued working for change until she died. Educated in the North at progressive schools, she chose to return south to her beloved Goldsboro, North Carolina, after finishing college. Once home, she earned the nickname "Federation Gertie" for her passion for civic reform. She fought tirelessly for women's rights, labor reform, and desegregation. Weil inspired me because she was a bold challenger and a natural organizer who loved discussion and debate. As I worked on this piece, I grew to feel that I knew her personally. She physically resembled my grandmother, who also attended college in the same era. Her activities were also very similar to my mother's crusades for the Equal Rights Amendment and social reform. Gertrude Weil was from an affluent Jewish family, which allowed her to have a privileged white lifestyle. She was quite striking physically, and the pictures I could find often showed her beautifully dressed. Even though she was quite humble, her natural leadership impulses always put her in the center of organizing and speaking, so I chose to have her front and center, looking directly at the audience. The women in the piece are from her graduating class at Smith College, and the "Votes for Women" button is based on a real brass button from the era. This piece is dye painted on cotton with thickened dyes and then machine quilted with hundreds of different colors of thread. I created a warm gray as the base because it looked like the old photos that inspired me.

Hollis Chatelain is an internationally recognized artist specializing in textile painting. Her work addresses challenging social and environmental themes, with dye-painted scenes of multicultural life conveying the untold stories of women, children, families, and the environment. She is inspired by her dreams, her experiences from life in Africa, and her passion for fighting for social reform since her teenage years. www.hollisart.com

Woman has a deep, intuitive, d ... nse of justice.

We Abolition Women are turning the world upside down.

Shin-hee Chin

MY WORK PORTRAYS THE COURAGE AND HUMANITY OF THE GRIMKÉ sisters, who are considered "the first American female advocates of abolition and women's rights." Though born into a slaveholding family in South Carolina, the two sisters, Sarah M. Grimké (1792–1873) and Angelina E. Grimké (1805–1879), dedicated their entire lives to addressing the injustice of enslavement and women's subjugation through lectures and education. They are credited as seeing the women's rights issue as a human rights issue. My work, *Grimké Sisters*, attempts to highlight women's independence and creativity that refuse to be restricted by old customs, prejudice, and discrimination. The overall structure of the work, as well as my techniques, have an important meaning as a compositional device and as a creative activity. The oval shape is used as a marker of social and cultural constriction imposed on females during the Victorian era. Simultaneously, the oval shape also symbolizes the egg from which a new life emerges. The slow and repetitive nature of my technique reenacts the creative process of birthing as well. I appropriate and valorize so-called "feminine" materials such as threads, fabric, and clothing, along with random stitching, through which one can see the complexly interwoven and intricately entangled thread covering the work. I intentionally use the different values of red, including white, pink, red, crimson, maroon, and black for my portraits of Grimké sisters. Through the gradation of color, I intend to delineate the slow but steady processes of expanding human freedom and equality. I use white-to-black-graduated oval frames for their quotes: "Woman has a deep, intuitive, divine sense of justice" (Sarah Grimké); "We abolition women are turning the world upside down" (Angelina Grimké).

Shin-hee Chin is a fiber/mixed-media artist and professor of the Visual Art Department at Tabor College. Chin's work has been exhibited nationally and internationally, including Washington, Tokyo, Hampton, Geneva, Tainan, and Seoul. She has taught drawing, painting, color theory, and mixed media and was elected as Distinguished Faculty in 2008. Influenced by feminist traditions, Christian spirituality, and Eastern philosophy, Chin has created a coherent narrative addressing complex issues of the female body, cultural identity, cultural hybridity, and sense of belonging. www.shinheechin.com

MARRIED TO DAVID WRIGHT   BROUGHT ATTRACTIVE BLEND OF JUDGEMENT, HUMOR AND PRACTICALITY   BORN A QUAKER

BORN CHRISTMAS DAY 1806

WELCOMED BLACK FRIENDS FREDERICK DOUGLAS AND HARRIET TUBMAN TO HER HOME

SISTER OF LUCRETIA MOTT.

GOOD FRIENDS WITH SUSAN B. ANTHONY & ELIZABETH CADDY STANTON

PEOPLE LOVE TO LAUGH   MOTHER OF 7 CHILDREN

PRESIDENT OF NATIONAL WOMAN SUFFRAGE ASSOCIATION

FRIEND OF FREDERICK DOUGLAS FOR ABOLITION OF SLAVERY AND HAD ARTICLES IN HIS PAPER THE NORTH STAR

Cochran

Jane Burch Cochran

I CHOSE MARTHA WRIGHT AS MY SUBJECT BECAUSE SHE WAS THE SISTER of suffragist Lucretia Mott and was also active in women's rights, although not as well known. I discovered that Wright's first husband was Peter Pelham from Kentucky, which is where I live. He died two years after their marriage, but she did have a son by him. I found a book about Martha Wright written by Sherry Penney and James Livingston, *A Very Dangerous Woman: Martha Wright and Women's Rights.* She was born a Quaker but left the Quaker religion and lived her life around Boston. She married David Wright, a lawyer, by whom she had six children, and was married to him until her death in 1875.

Along with several other women, Wright and her sister organized the historic 1848 Seneca Falls Convention. Wright was the secretary and didn't think she could speak in public. But she overcame that fear and not only spoke but also became known for her quick wit and writing. She was serving as president of the National Woman Suffrage Association when she died in 1875. On the cover of the book was a photograph of Martha Wright, on which I based my quilt. She seemed to wear dark, conservative clothing yet had a fanciful bonnet. I love to make patchwork that is random (not using a pattern), and used lots of darker colors for my quilt. I also added red, white, and blue patchwork along with a small American flag. I appliquéd with seed beads and bugle beads, and I used buttons to attach the batting and backing to the quilt top. Around the edges I stamped a few statements about her amazing life.

Jane Burch Cochran graduated from Centre College in Danville, Kentucky, in 1965. She moved to Cincinnati, Ohio, where she had a day job and studied painting at the Cincinnati Art Academy at night. She made her first large quilt in 1985, which made it into Quilt National. *Her quilts are highly embellished with buttons, beads, etc. Cochran's works are in numerous private and museum collections, including the Smithsonian (Renwick), National Quilt Museum, and the National Underground Freedom Center in Cincinnati.*

Sandy Curran

SHE HAS COME DOWN THROUGH HISTORY WITHOUT A NAME, ONLY AN image, a symbol of the sacrifice and bravery of the women called suffragists. She sits alone in a cell, bombed by sympathizers who tried to release the women imprisoned for asking for the right to vote; asking to have a say in the country and the world they lived in. The bombs broke the glass in the window, but the prison bars withstood the blast. So, she sits, patient and forlorn in prison, so that I, a hundred years later, could have a voice, could have an opinion that matters, could vote. And I have this to offer her: in my life, and I am no longer young, I have *never* missed a vote. From the first year I was old enough, I have never, not once, taken the right she won for me for granted. I have been sick, away from home, extremely busy—but I have always found a way to vote. Her bravery, suffering, and sacrifice were not in vain. I have honored her.

Sandy Curran began quilting in 1998, with a Baltimore Album appliquéd and quilted by hand. A cheerful obsession ensued. It took only two years for her to move from traditional appliqué to a completely innovative approach, but still with hand appliqué and quilting. Eventually, in order to tackle the designs she wanted, machine work became necessary, and later fusing and painting. A love of animals, fear for our planet, frustration with aging, love of color, and empathy for people in pain are her driving forces.

Ree Fagan

MY NEPHEW AND I WERE PLAYING OUR USUAL SATURDAY MORNING game of billiards and talking about the suffrage exhibit. While throwing around quilt ideas, I spoke of the force-feeding and jail time that some of the suffragists endured. He said, "Why don't you celebrate the women that were not militant?" It sounded good to me, and *Everyday Women Rallying for Suffrage* was born, to highlight the women who ran their households, raised their children, supported their husbands, and participated in the suffrage movement, not behind the podium but in the audience—our unsung heroes. It took more than eighty years for the Nineteenth Amendment to pass. In thinking how best to express the time frame, I chose hairstyles and hats during that period, knowing they would change. My research used books on historical fashions, theatrical costumes, women of Appalachia, fashion illustration, and historical quilt makers. The design of this quilt was done using technology. The background of the quilt is a thread design that was enlarged and colored in a gradient. Next I drew the faces, scanning them into the software and placing them on top of the colored threadwork. This process created a file that was then printed digitally on cotton sateen. Free-motion stitching finished it off, along with a silk tucked border.

Ree Fagan is a fiber artist who participates in textile-related competitions in the US and abroad. Notably, she has been a finalist several times at the Houston Quilt Festival, won Best Use of Thread at MQX Festival, won multiple ribbons at the Vermont Quilt Festival, and was a finalist for Viewer's Choice at Quilt National. Her work has been displayed in museums and galleries, including the Morristown Museum and the New England Quilt Museum. www.Reefagan.com

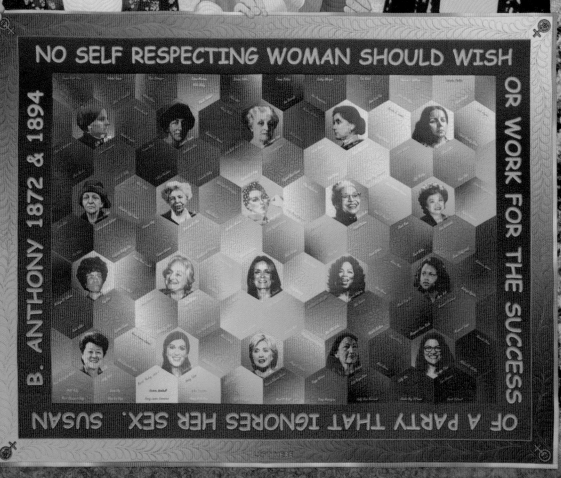

NO SELF RESPECTING WOMAN SHOULD WISH

OR WORK FOR THE SUCCESS

B. ANTHONY 1872 & 1894

OF A PARTY THAT IGNORES HER SEX.   SUSAN

Caryl Bryer Fallert-Gentry

THE INSPIRATION FOR *FIRST LADIES* WAS A JUNE 2, 1920, PHOTO, IN WHICH six officers of the National Woman's Party stand in Washington, DC, holding a banner with a quote by Susan B. Anthony. It reminded me of quilters holding up a quilt for "show and tell," so I designed a *Grandmother's Flower Garden* quilt with the quote in the border. In the hexagons, I decided to depict some of the women who have moved forward the cause of women's rights, and human rights in general, in the century since the ratification of the Nineteenth Amendment. After much research, I compiled a list of 162 women who accomplished important firsts in our country in the last one hundred years. I depicted three of the women holding the banner, and twenty others I considered to be the most significant, making digital drawings of each one. I chose at least one or two from each decade. In the other hexagons are the names of the other 139 first ladies. Although some of the names may not be familiar, each accomplished an important political or human rights first for her gender, faith, or ethnicity, including two major congressional firsts from the election that was current at the time the quilt was under construction. The quilt was designed on the computer, with individual parts printed by Spoonflower. In the sky fabric is an image of the Capitol, which can be seen only from a distance. Knowing that many of the names would be unfamiliar, I made an alphabetical list of the 162 first ladies and their accomplishments. The quilt within the quilt was constructed separately, and when it is lifted, the list can be found underneath. The colors of the hexagons are arranged in a gradation of rainbow colors, representing our diversity. The images of the twenty women are arranged in chronological order.

Caryl Bryer Fallert-Gentry is internationally recognized for her art quilts, which have appeared in hundreds of national and international exhibitions, collections, and publications. Honors include 100 Best Quilts of the 20th Century, Silver Star (lifetime achievement) Award, and selection as one of the thirty most influential quilt makers in the world. For thirty years, Fallert-Gentry lectured and taught in eleven countries around the world. Now retired from teaching, she continues to share her knowledge through free publications on her website. www.bryerpatch.com

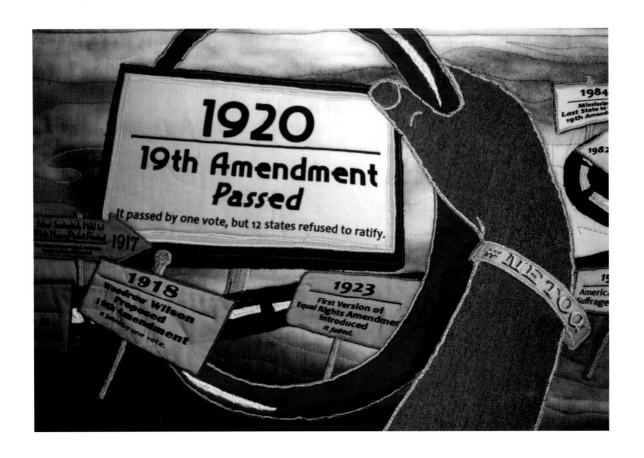

Jenny Bowker Cochran | Navigating the Legislative Highway (2018), 17 × 45 in.

Jayne Bentley Gaskins

AS I BEGAN RESEARCHING THE NINETEENTH AMENDMENT, I QUICKLY realized that this subject encompasses far more than just women's right to vote. It ties into all rights for women, as well as voting rights for all people. To paint a full picture, I couldn't highlight legislative milestones leading to the ratification of this amendment without acknowledging both state and federal voting legislation for blacks and Native Americans. With it all laid out on a timeline, we can see just how far the United States progressed in fewer than 150 years, from the dark early days of slavery and repression to this breakthrough legislation. But it wasn't enough. Native Americans still did not have the right to vote, and both women and other people of color were still far from equal to their white male counterparts. The Nineteenth Amendment set the stage for subsequent legal milestones affording justice and equality to women and all people of color. Follow this winding but very progressive road forward to today, and you can see how much more progress was made in only one hundred years. We've come a very long way, but have we reached total equality? No, and we likely won't for many years to come. But this amendment serves as a beacon of light urging us on for future generations. I created the entire design—dark road to bright future—using digital art and then appliquéd the individual pieces. The #MeToo bracelet was included to show that we most definitely have more miles to travel on this highway.

Gaskins's work has been exhibited in galleries and museums throughout the world and can be found in both private and museum collections as well as in numerous publications. She is a Juried Artist Member in Studio Art Quilt Associates and currently serves on the Board of Directors. Gaskins, who holds a BFA and an MBA, left a successful career in communications to pursue her love of art, where her imagination takes her places she never knew existed. www.jaynegaskins.com

Patricia Kennedy-Zafred

AS AN ARTIST WHO WORKS WITH PHOTOGRAPHIC IMAGES, I DISCOVERED many possibilities when choosing the concept and direction of this piece. In reviewing countless images of leaders within the suffragist movement, my attention was captured instead by local and regional leaders, and the women who followed them, most of their names remaining anonymous. Jessie Stubbs and "General" Rosalie Jones led suffragist marches to Albany, New York, and Washington, DC, their photo captured by Bain News Service. They appear proud and delighted, holding the American flag, with "Votes for Women" sashes emblazoned across their bodies. This image was simply irresistible. As a Pennsylvania resident, the image of the Pennsylvania "pickets" who marched to Washington in 1917, captured by Harris & Ewing Inc., was incredibly appealing.

The number of women in the original photo is actually larger than my design permitted, and has been cropped. Every woman in the photo featured clear and determined facial expressions; they were young, middle aged, and older yet found a common bond in this singular political effort. These were the unnamed heroes of the suffragist movement, who left their husbands and families to support an important cause, not unlike the women's marches of today. The photographs featured in my quilt, courtesy of the Library of Congress, are silkscreened on hand-dyed fabric, with news articles from the period added as accents. Choosing the coloration of the dyes was tricky, since it was not my desire to print on pink, the identifiable color of current women's political efforts. After several experiments in the dye buckets, I chose shades of blue, not only because I believed the tones best featured the black ink of the silkscreened images, but also because these women were encroaching into male territory, pushing their ideals into liberal states of blue. These women were brave, resilient, proud, and joyous, and I also sense in these images their mutual delight and camaraderie.

Patricia Kennedy-Zafred has been telling stories through the medium of textiles and art quilts for well over twenty years. Her work has been exhibited nationally and internationally and has been published in books and magazines throughout her career, most recently in Art Quilts Unfolding *(Schiffer Publishing, 2018). Her art is part of the permanent collection of the State Museum of Pennsylvania in Harrisburg, the Textile Museum in Washington, DC, and the San Jose Museum of Quilts & Textiles, as well as multiple private collections.*

Lovely Belva Lockwood, the Presidential Candidate.

Jill Kerttula

DURING HILLARY CLINTON'S RUN FOR PRESIDENT OF THE UNITED States in 2016, I saw a mention that she was not actually the first woman to run for president. In 1884 at age fifty-three, long before women had the right to vote, Belva Lockwood ran a nationwide campaign as a presidential candidate for the Equal Rights Party. As she said in one interview, "I cannot vote, but I can be voted for." As the first woman allowed to practice at the bar of the Supreme Court, she knew the constitutionality of her endeavor. There had been other fledgling campaigns supported by suffragist and prohibition groups, but none with the reach, support, and credibility of Belva Lockwood. The Equal Rights Party was formed by a group disillusioned with the lack of support that women's rights were receiving from the Republican Party. Lockwood's candidacy, however, was not a single-issue platform, and her inclusion of many issues made her unacceptable to some in the suffragist movement, who accused her of having a campaign that merely mirrored the male candidates. The campaign and press ephemera used in my piece may focus on her gender, but the press used strong satire and ridicule on all candidates at that time, suggesting that Belva Lockwood was seen as a legitimate candidate. These artifacts of her political life struck me as both graphically interesting and telling in the way that a woman candidate was viewed in the 1880s. It also struck me how little has changed with our politics in the subsequent years. In the largest image you can see all of the "baggage" a woman candidate was thought to bring with her in her quest to launch a campaign. The center smaller image depicts a man hiding under her skirts. The cover of *Puck* shows Lockwood and another candidate as comic performers. I had the images reproduced onto chiffon, tea-stained the fabric, and then added color with additional layers of fabric and stitching above and below the images.

Jill Kerttula is an artist in Charlottesville, Virginia, with a studio in the McGuffey Art Center. She brings together in her work her previous vocation as a design professional and her avocations of photography and stitching. To achieve her complex textures, she uses a variety of conventional and unconventional materials, and both hand and machine stitching. Working full-time on her fiber art has brought Kerttula recognition in many national and international exhibitions, including the 2019 Quilt National. www.jillkerttula.com

Pat Kumicich

I LOVE MUSIC WITH LYRICS THAT TELL A STORY. FOR THIS PROJECT, I was fortunate to find a book devoted to suffragist sheet music, with songs that date back to as early as 1875. The lyrics were an eye opener for me. When I first got involved with this project, I thought the suffragist movement was strictly about the right to vote. Nothing could be further from the truth! The battle to win the right to vote for women in the United States was hard fought not only by women, but by men as well. Generations of women stood together peacefully demanding freedom, equal rights, and emancipation for all. Our vote is our voice. I am grateful to my sisters and brothers of yore who fought long and hard so that our voices could be heard today. Their efforts to succeed set the stage for grassroots efforts to come, proving that determined citizens can achieve change. Actual book pages make up the background of my quilt. Cotton fabric was painted or stenciled as well as digitally printed. A combination of hand embroidery and machine quilting completed the work.

Pat Kumicich is a Florida-based artist who creates contemporary quilts. She focuses her attention on social issues, mass-media news coverage of events that often feature women, and women she knows personally or creates in her imagination. She says that working in the art quilt medium allows her to express her innermost feelings about our world, the times we live in, and the human condition. Kumicich loves making her mark with needle and thread. www.patkumicich.com

John Lefelhocz

I STARTED BRAINSTORMING FOR THIS ARTWORK BY LOOKING AT existing suffrage-related quilts and was drawn to an example from the late 1800s (maker unknown). This red, white, and blue flag-inspired historic quilt is in the collection of the Museum of Fine Arts, Boston. Also appealing to me was a political cartoon by Henry Mayer from 1915, titled "The Awakening." This image showed Lady Liberty marching "Votes for Women" across a map of the United States. After some internal debate, I decided that I would be comfortable creating a remake of the 1800s quilt, incorporating a hand-stitched Lady Liberty image. The remake would be similar to the way a filmmaker or musician remakes a movie or song. My intent was to copy the original and to include some new elements that reference and encourage a dialogue about our current times. Further inspiration came from this Elizabeth Cady Stanton quote: "The moment we begin to fear the opinions of others and hesitate to tell the truth that is in us, and from motives of policy are silent when we should speak, the divine floods of light and life no longer flow into our souls." The big question to myself was how to blend into my version the idea that hesitation to act on one's convictions can prevent the flow of "divine floods of light and life" into our souls. My answer was to include backlighting that uses a nonrepeating generative animation sequence with range detectors. The colors displayed by my quilt come from a system of autonomy through an algorithm using math and machine logic. Although the colors shown come from a rigid rule structure, the viewer still has the ability to take part and ultimately change and enhance the colors presented, according to where they stand in relation to the quilt via deeds (not words).

John Lefelhocz is an American conceptual artist primarily known for his works in the textile arts, specifically art quilts. He studied mixed media at Ohio University. Since college, he has owned and operated Cycle Path Bicycle Shop in Athens, Ohio, at the same time establishing himself as an artist. His art gained higher recognition in the late 1990s. Lefelhocz has subsequently shown his works throughout the US and abroad. www.juxtapassion.com

LUCY STONE
AUGUST 13, 1818 - OCTOBER 18, 1893
LUCY STONE WAS THE FIRST WOMAN
FROM MASSACHUSETTS TO EARN A
COLLEGE DEGREE. LUCY AND HER
HENRY BLACKWELL WROTE THEIR OWN
EGALITARIAN WEDDING VOWS
PENNED A FAMOUS PROTEST AGAINST
PATRIARCHAL LAWS & CUSTOMS
GOVERNING MARRIAGE. SHE fought
AN UPHILL BATTLE TO CONTINUE USING
HER OWN SURNAME. ALL HER LIFE
LUCY STONE STOOD AGAINST
INEQUALITIES

Susan Lenz | *Lucy Stone* (2018). 3-D work, diptych: open, 26 × 40 in.; closed, 26 × 20 × 3 in.

Exterior (covers) of Susan Lenz | Lucy Stone

Susan Lenz

FROM THE BEGINNING, I KNEW THAT I WANTED TO CREATE A HINGED work that referenced antique daguerreotypes. This early photographic process employed an iodine-sensitized silver plate and mercury vapor to create a very fragile, mirrorlike surface with extremely accurate and sharp details. Because the plates were so vulnerable to damage, most were presented in special folding cases, often with velvet liners and ornate clasps. The process was named for its inventor, Louis Jacques Mandé Daguerre. The daguerreotype was the first publicly available photographic process, and pretty much the only one used for personal portraiture from 1840 to 1860. Many of the early suffragists had such images made, and most are available through the Library of Congress, a source for high-resolution images in the public domain. The Library of Congress owns seven featuring Lucy Stone; I selected the one I liked best. However, I'd like to clarify one important thing! I did *not* select Lucy Stone just because I found a high-resolution, copyright-free image of an original daguerreotype. I did not select her because she was the first woman from Massachusetts to earn a college degree (though I very much like that fact!). I selected Lucy Stone because she refused to give up her surname upon marriage and because she and her husband, Henry, wrote their own, egalitarian wedding vows and penned a famous protest against patriarchal laws and customs governing marriage. Lucy Stone stood against all inequalities. She was an abolitionist and a great public orator and was part of the nineteenth-century "triumvirate" of women's suffrage and feminism along with Susan B. Anthony and Elizabeth Cady Stanton. The more I read about Lucy Stone, the more I knew I wanted to stitch her portrait more than any other suffragist's picture.

As a fiber and installation artist, Susan Lenz uses a multidisciplinary approach to express her feminist viewpoint and desire to leave a lasting legacy through her art. Lenz's works have appeared in national publications, juried exhibitions, and the Philadelphia Museum of Art and the Smithsonian Craft Shows. She has been featured on two quilting television programs, on a South Carolina educational channel, and in international invitational opportunities. Her solo installations have been mounted all over the country. www.susanlenz.com

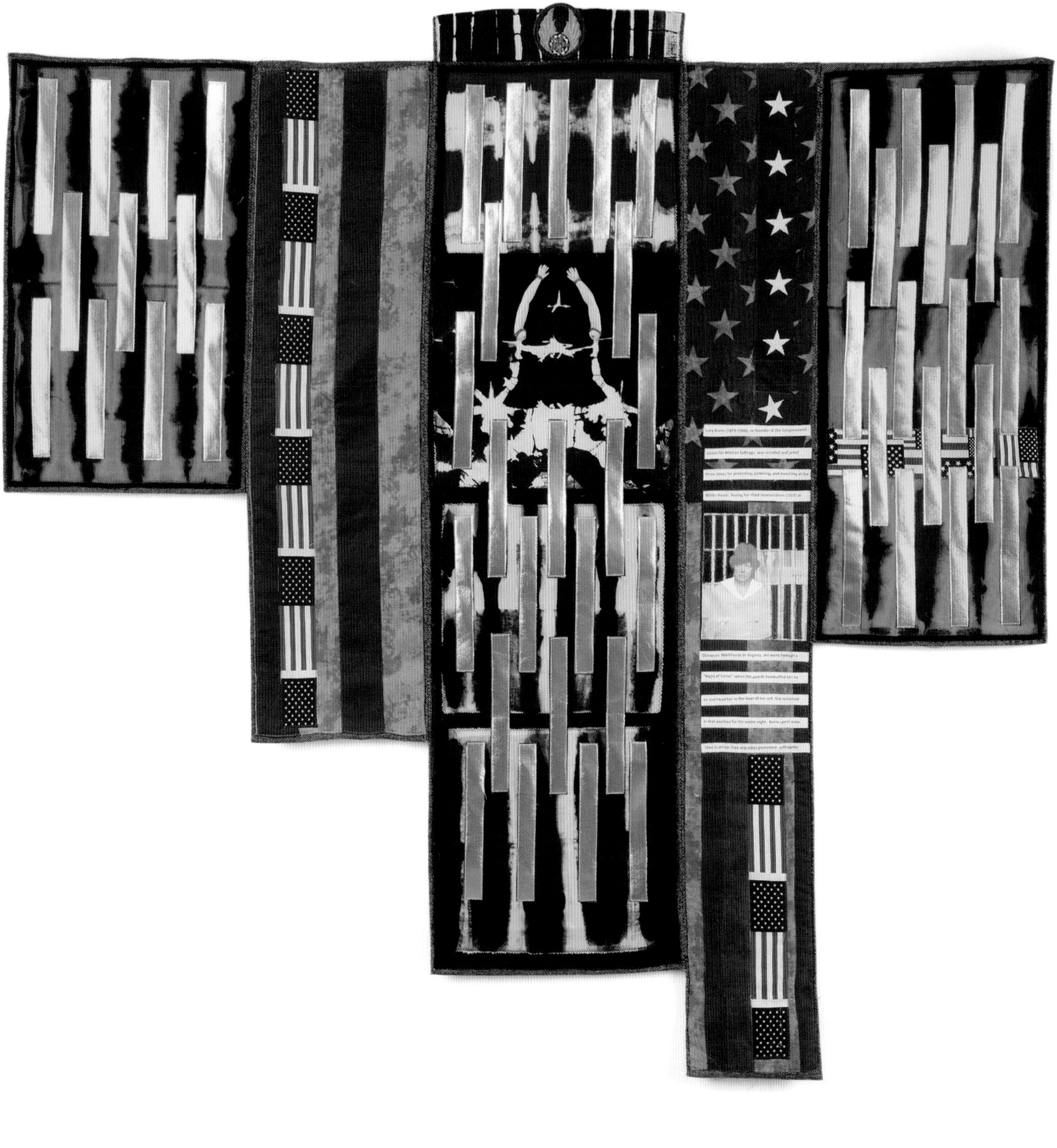

Patricia Malarcher | *Homage to Lucy Burns* (2019): 53 × 54.75 in. | *Photo by Peter Jacobs*

Patricia Malarcher

AS I BEGAN MY RESEARCH ON THE SUFFRAGISTS FOR *DEEDS NOT WORDS*, I was looking for an aspect of the movement that inspired a visual interpretation of historical content. I found my subject when I began to read about the suffragists who were arrested and imprisoned, and of the harsh treatment they received. Immediately I envisioned a quilt with black-and-white stripes as a dominant pattern. I'd been working with discharge—a process by which color is removed from dyed fabric—and decided that bleached-out vertical lines on black cotton would establish the grim mood I wanted to convey. That was my starting point. Further research brought Lucy Burns to my attention. A high-spirited organizer in the National Woman's Party, she was arrested three times for protesting, picketing, and marching at the White House. During her third imprisonment at the notorious Occoquan Workhouse in Virginia, she suffered a "night of terror" handcuffed to an overhead vertical bar in her cell after being brutally beaten by the guards. My piece contains an image of Lucy Burns in jail and a symbolic representation of her ordeal. It also references the American flag, since the goal of the movement was access to the privileges of full citizenship. Although the subject is dark, there also is a hint of the ultimate victory within reach but not yet attained.

Patricia Malarcher is a studio artist who produces wall pieces and artist books. She has exhibited nationally and in Europe, Asia, and Africa. The recipient of three Artist Fellowships from the NJ State Council on the Arts, she has shown in 20 solo and numerous group exhibitions. Collections representing her include the Museum of Arts and Design, Newark Museum, Cleveland Art Museum, International Quilt Study Center & Museum, and several corporate and private collections. She was editor of Surface Design Journal, *1993–2011.*

Therese May, I Vote for You (2018, Sojourner Truth), 67 × 72 in | Photo by Ian May

Therese May

SOJOURNER TRUTH'S STORY IS A METAPHOR FOR THE LIVES OF MANY women today, which is the reason why I portrayed her as a vibrant modern figure. Although as her adventure unfolded there was no voting for women, she found ways of voting for *herself* by walking away from slavery and finding a life of freedom doing the work of a minister and giving lectures about women's suffrage. The "Vote for You" panels bordering this quilt convey the message of following the powerful inner guidance that Sojourner Truth inspired. The stitched words on her face are Love, Women's Rights, Save the Children, Loving Kindness, All One, Love One Another, and Speak Your Word—the latter stitched onto her lips, suggesting that anyone has this power. "Walk Away from Slavery One Step at a Time" can be interpreted as the encouragement to free oneself from any kind of bondage. The idea of writing on her face was inspired by the *Time* magazine cover of the face of Christine Blasey Ford, who in 2018 bravely stood up for herself by testifying about alleged sexual abuse by Brett Kavanaugh. Even though he was confirmed for the Supreme Court, a valuable step was taken for women's equality. Sojourner Truth also stood up in a similar way, when her son was sold back into slavery after slavery was abolished. She walked barefoot many miles to the courthouse and insisted on her son's release. She won and may have been the first black woman in the US to stand up, take a case to court, and win. Sojourner Truth was a beautiful and self-assured heroic woman who stepped out of the worst of circumstances and moved forward in life to solve extreme dilemmas one at a time, including a woman's right to vote. The crown on her head signifies the brilliance of her heart, of which she took ownership.

One of the pioneers of the Art Quilt movement, Therese May began creating quilts in 1965. Her work has been exhibited worldwide, including at the Louvre and the Smithsonian, as well as being published in many books and magazines. Her art quilts are part of private and public collections, including museums and hospitals. She has taught for quilting guilds across the nation and at the college level, including the Cleveland Institute of Art and the University of California. www.theresemay.com

Pixeladies

KATHARINE DEXTER MCCORMICK IS THE MOST COMPELLING, multifaceted person we had never heard of before we started doing research on influential women. McCormick, one of America's great philanthropists, never sought recognition, but she deserves it. McCormick was the second woman to graduate from the Massachusetts Institute of Technology (MIT), majoring in biology in 1904. She had the requirement that women always wear hats rescinded for the chemistry lab (which is why we love this image of her in a hat so much). McCormick never lost touch with her MIT roots, financing the first female dormitory at MIT. Opened in 1963, it provided rooms for two hundred women. Women now make up almost half of the undergraduates at MIT. McCormick was an ardent activist for the suffragist movement. She served as treasurer and vice president of the National American Woman Suffrage Association (NAWSA). After meeting Margaret Sanger in 1917, she supported Sanger's work on contraception. McCormick even smuggled more than one thousand birth-control diaphragms from Europe for Sanger's clinic while they were still illegal in the United States. These diaphragms were sewn into her clothing, making our fiber medium conducive to a hidden homage (Can you spot the two diaphragms we sewed into this quilt?). Convinced that women's sovereignty was based on their ability to control birth, McCormick almost single-handedly financed the development of the birth-control pill, which the FDA approved in 1960. To construct this quilt, we collaged words and phrases cut from magazines and newspapers, then printed the image onto cotton fabric, using fiber-reactive dyes. We machine stitched the quilt, adding the boa (printed onto silk and cotton and cut into strips) to create the three-dimensional effect, because we think everyone should wear a boa, as McCormick does in the original image. The background shows an excerpt from her acceptance speech as member at large at the 1911 NAWSA Convention.

The Pixeladies are Deb Cashatt and Kris Sazaki. Collaborating since 2003, they use the computer to draft compositions, which they collage with texts and phrases cut from magazines and newspapers. For the Pixeladies, the texts have literal meaning as well as aesthetic value. The Pixeladies often take everyday objects and imbue them with political or social meaning, working primarily in fiber because of its tactile nature. And they like to sew. www.pixeladies.com

VOTES FOR WOMEN

WHEN THE BALLOT IS PUT INTO THE HANDS OF THE AMERICAN WOMAN. THE WORLD IS GOING

VOTES FOR WOMEN

TO GET A CORRECT ESTIMATE OF THE NEGRO WOMAN. IT WILL FIND HER A TOWER OF STRENGTH.

VOTES FOR WOMEN

Arturo Alonzo Sandoval

THIS QUILT WAS INSPIRED BY MY FRIEND NECIA DESIREE HARKLESS, whose mother, Ethel Williams Harkless, was a Detroit suffragist. Internet articles disclosed the awful truth that a "white separatist" attitude by suffrage leaders rendered nearly invisible those black women who labored in the suffragist movement. This racism tightened its grip on the fight for women's suffrage. White women wanted the vote, but many of them did not want to include blacks in their marches; if blacks did march, they were to be at the back. This memorial quilt pays homage to each African-American suffragist and their valiant efforts in helping push through the Nineteenth Amendment to the US Constitution. The women included in my quilt are from the list of Dr. Rosalyn Terborg-Penn's works, edited by Edith Mayo, titled "African American Women Leaders in the Suffrage Movement," and I added Necia's mother to this list (see appendix 2). Black suffragists were not given their rightful place among the main women's suffrage movement, so many are detailed here, including "colored women clubs" of the period. The paraphrased text is by Nannie Helen Burroughs. The design for my quilt takes on the form of a poster or banner. The addition of stars and stripes and sewing thread in American flag colors adds a patriotic tone to the composition. The four corners cry out "VOTES FOR WOMEN" and add visual weight. The vinyl digital image is punctuated and allows the middle Mylar layer to show through.

Arturo Alonzo Sandoval, emeritus professor, is known internationally for his innovative mixed-media fiber art. Sandoval received two NEA fellowships and three Al Smith Kentucky Art Council Fellowships and is a fellow of the American Craft Council. He pursues the cutting edge, transforming industrial, linear, recycled materials. His art, inspired by textile and computer technology, uses pattern, text, sewing, and interlacing to create unique graphic-art expressions. "Work produces results" is his art philosophy mantra.

Joan Schulze

THE MYTH OF LADY GODIVA RIDING THROUGH THE TOWN CENTER TO suspend taxes has been an inspiration for works of art by many artists since the eleventh century. Leading the Woman Suffrage Association's parade in Washington, DC, in March 1913 was Inez Milholland Boissevain, seated on a white horse. Each woman, centuries apart, rode a horse for a cause–Lady Godiva to affect the lives of ordinary people, and Boissevain for women's right to vote. I began exploring ways to use this imagery for my quilt. A march? A parade? How best to bring people together for the cause of women's rights? In my research, these two stories struck a chord: One woman on a horse in the eleventh century, who may, in turn, have inspired the horsewoman Boissevain to dress in white on a white horse for the 1913 parade. Towering over the marchers and parade goers, she would naturally capture people's attention and imagination, as did Lady Godiva riding naked. Leap forward one hundred years. Women are still marching together, arm in arm, showing a united front. Progress is slow. Over time, events have had a way of galvanizing the community of women and men to move the conversation. The message is still clear. *Together* things can change. The making of a quilt is slow work: capturing the idea, finding the right compilation of materials, creating a design, and then translating thoughts and ideas into reality can consume days and nights. Each part of the whole is important. To keep focused, I thought about the women who, over time, have challenged each other to overcome obstacles and collectively create not only the possibility of change but also change itself. *Together*, mountains are moved.

Awarded the 2017 Distinguished Woman Artist by the Council of 100, Fresno Art Museum, California, Joan Schulze has other singular honors, including a 2016 solo exhibition, Shenzhen Art Museum; Tsinghua University Art Museum, Beijing, China, 2018; and her retrospective exhibition Poetic License: The Art of Joan Schulze at the San Jose Museum of Quilts & Textiles, 2010. Her work is held in public collections, including recent acquisitions by the Newark Museum, Racine Art Museum, and Fresno Art Museum. Schulze maintains studios in San Francisco and Sunnyvale, California. www.joan-of-arts.com

Let men be compelled to wear our dress for awhile and we should soon hear them advocating a change.

Amelia Bloomer

Robin Schwalb

WHEN I WAS A CHILD, MY FAMILY CALLED GIRLS' UNDERPANTS "bloomers." I can't recall that we ever mentioned or were even aware of the origin of that name. I now know that Amelia Jenks Bloomer (1818–1894) became associated with the women's clothing-reform style known as bloomers because of her early and strong advocacy. It was inspiring to learn that her work on behalf of women's rights and temperance led her to become the first woman to own, operate, and edit a newspaper for women: *The Lily*, whose title is commemorated in the present-day *Washington Post*'s online feature for women. I based the triple images of my quilt on an 1851 illustration of Amelia Bloomer wearing the bloomer costume. The colors of the American suffragists were white, gold, and purple–symbolizing purity, life, and loyalty–so I colored my three Amelias accordingly. The background is a repeating dictionary definition of bloomers that I silkscreened onto a subtly printed fabric. For the figures and the border text, I used a combination of appliqué and reverse appliqué by machine, using a fusible web, and then did zigzag stitching around every raw edge. I quilted this piece by hand. Part of the quilting design in the borders was inspired by the title art of *The Lily* newspaper, which was published between 1849 and 1856. Although founded as a temperance newspaper, it gradually focused on women's rights, especially suffrage. When Bloomer and her family moved to Iowa in 1854 and she sold the newspaper to Mary Birdsall, it had more than six thousand subscribers across the country.

Robin Schwalb explores the rich variety of the written word in her graphically compelling quilts, balancing an appreciation of their abstract beauty with the desire to include the "found art" of relevant texts. This desire to use specific, personally meaningful images dictates a process-oriented approach. Schwalb transforms her basic material with photo silkscreen printing, stenciling, dyeing, and painting, in addition to the standard repertory of piecing, appliqué, and quilting.

Susan Shie

CHARLOTTE WOODWARD PIERCE IS MY SUFFRAGIST. I HEARD ABOUT her on National Public Radio and was intrigued about this youngest woman to attend the 1848 Seneca Falls Convention, at age eighteen. She was the only one of those women still alive when women won the right to vote in 1920. But at age ninety-one, she was bedfast and unable to go vote. I had not heard of her before, and very little was written about Pierce. I drew her from a photo but ad-libbed her sewing on a large man's glove. Because she hated not getting paid any wages, beyond room and board for sewing gloves all day, she pounced on the idea of a women's convention for improving our rights. Since 1998, I've been making my Kitchen Tarot deck quilts, so Charlotte Woodward Pierce is also the Knight of Potholders (coins), committed to making life better. Besides her, other women depicted here are Stacey Abrams, the Statue of Liberty, Rep. Shirley Chisholm, Hillary Clinton, Eleanor Roosevelt, and the 102 women of the 116th House of Representatives, elected in November 2018. These women of the new House of Representatives seemed perfect to go with my suffragist subject here, since they wore white on the night of the 2019 State of the Union speech to honor the suffragist movement. Because I was working on this piece while healing from a severely broken arm, I made this quilt smaller than usual and simplified my writing process, and it worked. I drew this whole-cloth piece freehand with my airbrush, then wrote on it with markers and pens since I can't use my AirPen until my arm is better. I sewed the quilt mostly by machine. I loved making this piece about so many powerful women, who all worked or are working for women's rights and human rights!

A lifelong Ohio artist, Susan Shie earned an MFA in 1986 from the School of Art of Kent State University and has been a professional artist and teacher since then. She added sewing to her paintings as a feminist statement in 1979, when Miriam Schapiro did an artist residence at the College of Wooster. Shie's work is both personal diary and social commentary, focusing on women, history, current events, ecology, peace, and healing. She teaches intuitive freehand drawing: "Everyone can draw!" www.turtlemoon.com

Sandra Sider

FRANCES ELLEN WATKINS HARPER (1825–1911) SPENT HER ENTIRE ADULT life struggling for racial equality as well as women's suffrage, with the former at the forefront of her efforts. "Bundle of Humanity" in my quilt comes from her 1866 speech at the Eleventh National Woman's Rights Convention, and the strength of her convictions can be felt in the core sentence of that speech: "We are all bound up together in one great bundle of humanity, and society cannot trample on the weakest and feeblest of its members without receiving the curse in its own soul." Other speakers that day included Susan B. Anthony, Lucretia Mott, and Elizabeth Cady Stanton. This event established Harper's prominence as an orator among feminist leaders, and she did not hesitate to criticize racist attitudes on the part of some women among the suffragists. By the time she was thirty, Harper was involved in the abolitionist movement, even residing for a while in an Underground Railroad station in Philadelphia. This amazing woman was also a literary phenomenon. Born into a free black family in Baltimore, Harper had the advantage of attending a relatively rigorous school directed by her uncle, the Reverend William Watkins, where she was taught biblical studies, the classics, and elocution. Another stroke of luck was that, as a teenager, she was employed by a family that owned a bookstore, and she was encouraged to read. That young woman went on to become one of the most popular African-American authors of the nineteenth century.

The texts on my quilt are from Harper's own poems and speeches, found in *A Brighter Coming Day*, edited by Frances Smith Foster (1990). The photo-transferred portrait of Harper was sourced from the Library of Congress.

Sandra Sider, a New York quilt artist since the early 1980s, holds an MA in art history from the Institute of Fine Arts, New York University, and taught art history and material culture at the college level from 2004 to 2014. She works mostly with photographic processes on fabric, especially cyanotype. Her quilts can be found in seven museum collections. www.sandrasider.com

Jane Addams

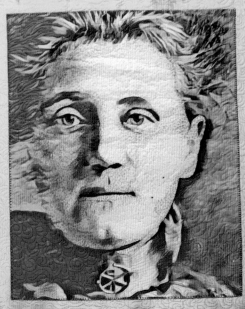

A Most Dangerous Woman

Laura Wasilowski

JANE ADDAMS (1860–1935) IS AN INSPIRATION TO ALL WHO WISH TO MAKE the world a better place. She was a social reformer, suffragist, feminist, pacifist, and winner of the Nobel Peace Prize in 1931. As cofounder of Hull House, a settlement house located in Chicago, Illinois, she focused on the needs of children, women, immigrants, and workers. Addams was a vocal fighter for the oppressed and marginalized. She advocated for public health reform, universal suffrage, child labor laws, and world peace. It was her crusade for peace during World War I that caught J. Edgar Hoover's attention. In 1915, she convened a women's conference in support of opposing the war. Although women did not yet have the vote, more than three thousand women attended the conference in Washington, DC. The federal government's newly enacted Sedition Act prohibited criticism of the war and America's preparation for it. Concerned about her ability to speak to the masses, Hoover, the founding director of the FBI, opened a file on Addams and called her "the Most Dangerous Woman in America." This most dangerous woman participated in the founding of the National Association for the Advancement of Colored People, the American Civil Liberties Union, and the Women's International League for Peace and Freedom. She also had a sense of humor. Here is a quote by Jane Addams from an address before the Chicago Political Equality League in 1897: "I am not one of those who believe–broadly speaking–that women are better than men. We have not wrecked railroads, nor corrupted legislatures, nor done many unholy things that men have done; but then we must remember that we have not had the chance." Jane Addams was dedicated to the betterment of humanity–truly a most dangerous and inspiring woman.

Laura Wasilowski creates hand-dyed fabrics and threads, pictorial art quilts, and free-form embroideries. Her whimsical textile pieces tell stories of family, friends, and home. They express her joy and love of making artwork. The artist is also a lecturer, quilt instructor, pattern designer, and author of Fanciful Stitches, Colorful Quilts *and* Joyful Stitching: Transform Fabric with Improvisational Embroidery. *www.artfabrik.com*

Hana Wilmarth | *Tour de Force* (2018, text of 19th Amendment), 45 × 34 in. | *Photo by Rick Wells*

Hope Wilmarth

BECAUSE HISTORY IS IMPORTANT TO ME, I CHOSE TO WRITE ABOUT IT as my celebration of the one hundredth year of women's suffrage. I especially hope that the words on the quilt will be read by my grandchildren, who have a legacy of strong, independent women as role models. The words of the Nineteenth Amendment, a grand tour de force, are brushed onto parchment-like cloth, in the midst of which stands the silhouette of a representational suffragist of the era. To her right, she looks at a timeline of events, written in small black letters. The timeline begins with the 1776 plea from Abigail Adams to her husband to "remember the ladies" when writing the Declaration of Independence. The timeline ends with ratification of the amendment in 1920. Behind the suffragist, written in small black letters, are names of suffragists on whose shoulders I stand. Women have made an impact on the ballot box since 1920. Our voices can and will be heard if we choose to continue to walk the path paved by the brave women who came before us.

Hope Wilmarth created her first art quilt in 2009, responding to a juried gallery call. The experience led her into the world of fiber artists, which continues to challenge, educate, and open new opportunities for her to explore surface design. Wilmarth's professional background is that of a registered nurse, during which time she enjoyed traditional quilting, calligraphy, embroidery, and other media that she now applies to her art. She is a published fiber artist, exhibiting nationally and internationally, and a Juried Artist Member of Studio Art Quilt Associates. www.hopewilmarth.com

The banner on the car reads: "WE DEMAND AMENDMENT TO THE UNITED STATES CONSTITUTION ENFRANCHISING WOMEN"

Martha Wolfe | *Sara Bard Field: Suffrage Envoy* (2019), 40 × 50 in.

Martha Wolfe

SARA BARD FIELD: SUFFRAGE ENVOY HONORS SUFFRAGIST SARA BARD Field and her cross-country automobile journey delivering a petition with more than five hundred thousand signatures supporting the Susan B. Anthony Amendment to Congress and President Woodrow Wilson. The petition was started in January 1915 by the Congressional Union for Women Suffrage (CU) at their "Freedom Booth" at the Panama-Pacific International Exhibition in San Francisco. In a gesture to heighten awareness of the movement, Alice Paul, cofounder of the CU, asked Field, a committed suffragist and human rights activist, to escort the petition across the US, hosting numerous parades, rallies, and speaking engagements along the way to publicize their cause and collect additional signatures. On September 16, 1915, the convoy, including Field, driver Maria Kinberg, and mechanic Ingeborg Kindstedt, departed San Francisco in their newly purchased Overland vehicle. On December 6, 1915, following an eventful three-month journey, the connvoy arrived in Washington, DC, met by hundreds of supporters on foot, in automobiles, and on horseback. Field addressed the crowd from the steps of the Capitol, and then they all marched to the White House, with the massive petition partially unrolled, where it was received by President Wilson. The work was created using photographs sourced from the Library of Congress as inspiration. The background was made from late-nineteenth-century fabrics. The quilt is layered with silk organza, and the raw-edge appliquéd figures in the foreground are collaged from charmeuse and dupioni silk, Japanese yarn-dyed cottons, and hand-dyed cottons. Because of my family relationship with Sara Bard Field, a piece of my grandmother's dress (Field's first cousin) was used to fashion her blouse. Field was also a poet, and I added her signature from a dedication in one of her first editions.

Martha Wolfe is a fiber artist living in Northern California. Her work has been published in numerous magazines and books and is held in public and private collections. Wolfe exhibits, teaches, and lectures worldwide. She is the founding member and curator of the international collaborative group Viewpoints 9, consisting of nine artists sharing a guided creative journey and exhibiting together. She currently serves on the Board of Directors of Studio Art Quilt Associates. www.marthawolfe.com

Adrienne Yorinks

I CREATED *RESISTANCE TO TYRANNY IS OBEDIENCE TO GOD* TWENTY-FIVE years ago to celebrate the seventy-fifth anniversary of women's suffrage. The title is a quote from Susan B. Anthony. I distinctly remember days in the library culling every book and article I could find on the suffrage movement. I was mesmerized by the strength and determination of the women participants, particularly Susan B. Anthony, Elizabeth Cady Stanton, and Sojourner Truth. During this time, I had the opportunity to visit the Women's Rights National Historical Park. Their exhibit focused on the first Woman's Rights Convention, held in Seneca Falls, New York, in 1848. I found a pamphlet containing the Declaration of Sentiments, written by Elizabeth Cady Stanton. Reading the declaration and seeing the names of the women and men who signed it, I knew that this text had to be the anchor of my work. I envisioned a monument in fabric to the women who had sacrificed so much for all of us. I used white-on-white fabric, with the text of the declaration printed on top to resemble marble. I used vintage fabrics spanning the years of the suffragist movement to connect to my photomontage. A favorite vintage fabric in the work is a quirky, pink background fabric with a woman in green carrying a gun. Pink is the predominant color because, as a child, I felt I was force-fed pink. It represented the stereotypical "feminine" attributes, so I used pink ironically to juxtapose the "girly" and "feminine" characteristics against the powerful, brilliant, and brave attributes these women actually possessed.

Adrienne Yorinks is a fiber artist whose work has been exhibited throughout the US and around the world. Described as an abstract expressionist, she is known for her bold sense of color and movement. She has created numerous private and public commissions, many depicting historical or commemorative themes produced via photo transfers. Yorinks has authored and illustrated several books, including The Last Will and Testament of an Extremely Distinguished Dog, *an essay written by Eugene O'Neill in 1949. www.adrienneyorinks.com*

List of Artists and Quilts in the Exhibition

Teresa Barkley
Tea Box to Ballot Box (2019), 74 × 58 in.
Photo by Jean Vong

Alice Beasley
She Refused to Walk Behind (2019, Ida Wells),
35.25 × 40 in.
Photo by Sibila Savage Photography

Maria Billings
Clara Foltz (2018), 64 × 25 in. (20 in. wide when
installed as column)
Photo by Visual Simplicity

Sue Bleiweiss
Nasty Women Keep Fighting (2018), 49 × 49 in.
Photo by the artist

Hollis Chatelain
Federation Gertie (2019), 57 × 51 in.
Photo by the artist

Shin-hee Chin
Grimké Sisters (2019), 64.5 × 56.5 in.
Photo by Jim Turner

Jane Burch Cochran
Martha Wright (2019), 58 × 42 in.
Photo by Pamela Braun

Sandy Curran
Honor Her (2019), 50 × 31 in.
Photo by the artist

Ree Fagan
Everyday Women Rallying for Women's Suffrage
(2019), 36 × 45 in.
Photo by Jeffrey Lomicka

Caryl Bryer Fallert-Gentry
First Ladies (2018), 63 × 56 in.
Photo by the artist

Jayne Gaskins
Navigating the Legislative Highway (2018),
17 × 45 in.
Photo by the artist

Patricia Kennedy-Zafred
No Shrinking Violets (2018), 61.5 × 45 in.
Photo by Larry Berman

Jill Kerttula
Belva Lockwood (2019), 43 × 33 in.
Photo by the artist

Pat Kumicich
Standing Together (2018), 37.5 × 56 in.
Photo by the artist

John Lefelhocz
Divine Floods of Light and Life (2019), 3-D work,
42 × 41 × 3 in.
Photo by the artist

Susan Lenz
Lucy Stone (2018), 3-D work, diptych: open,
26 × 40 in.; closed, 26 × 20 × 3 in.
Photo by the artist

Patricia Malarcher
Homage to Lucy Burns (2019), 53 × 54.75 in.
Photo by Peter Jacobs

Therese May
Vote for You (2018, Sojourner Truth), 67 × 72 in.
Photo by Ian May

Pixeladies
Katharine Dexter McCormick: Making Her Mark
(2019), 38 × 36 in.
Photo by Deb Cashatt

Arturo Alonzo Sandoval
Unsung Heroines of African-American Suffrage
(2019), 84 × 84 in.
Photo by Scott Walz

Joan Schulze
Together (2018), 36.5 × 52.5 in.
Photo by the artist

Robin Schwalb
Amelia Bloomer: Advocating a Change (2019), 48 × 48 in.
Photo by Jean Vong

Susan Shie
Charlotte: Knight of Potholders (coins) in the Kitchen Tarot
(2019), 58 × 59 in.
Photo by the artist

Sandra Sider
Frances Watkins Harper: "I Speak of Wrongs"
(2019), 32 × 33.5 × 1 in.
Photo by Deidre Adams

Laura Wasilowski
Jane Addams: A Most Dangerous Woman (2019),
46 × 37.5 in.
Photo by the artist

Hope Wilmarth
Tour de Force (2018, text of 19th Amendment),
45 × 34 in.
Photo by Rick Wells

Martha Wolfe
Sara Bard Field: Suffrage Envoy (2019), 40 × 50 in.
Photo by the artist

Adrienne Yorinks
Resistance to Tyranny Is Obedience to God (1995),
79 × 71 in.
Photo by Craig Dietrich

Quilt Artists at Work

WE WELCOME YOU INTO THE STUDIOS OF SEVERAL ARTISTS IN THE book who documented their works-in-progress for *Deeds not Words*. Each photograph represents months of designing, assembling, stitching, and finishing an art quilt for every maker represented here. Art quilts—also referred to as studio quilts or studio art quilts—are original visual works created with artistic intent, having a layered structure and stitching, or referencing stitching, either by hand or by machine. Essentially consisting of cloth, art quilts may be made of commercially printed fabrics or surface designs created by the artists through various techniques, and you will see several examples of the latter in the images to follow.

Pat Kumicich drawing a face for *Standing Together*

84

Kris Sazaki trimming *Katharine Dexter McCormick: Making Her Mark*

Deb Cashatt trimming *Katharine Dexter McCormick: Making Her Mark*

Caryl Bryer Fallert-Gentry drawing Alice Paul
Photo by Ron Gentry

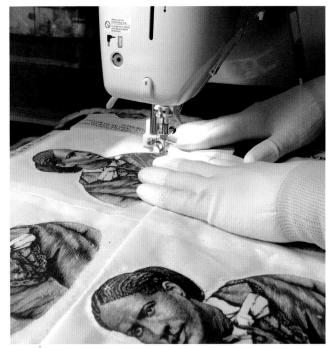

Sandra Sider quilting *Frances Watkins Harper: "I Speak of Wrongs"*

Susan Shie at work on *Charlotte: Knight of Potholders (coins) in the Kitchen Tarot*

Appendix 1

Caryl Bryer Fallert-Gentry

First Ladies

Women who were the first of their sex or ethnicity to do things that were previously done only by men or people of other ethnicity or sexual orientation, and notable women who moved equality forward for others in their generation

Aida Álvarez: first Hispanic woman to hold a cabinet-level position, 1997

Alice K. Kurashige: first Japanese American woman commissioned in the United States Marine Corps, 1964

Alice Paul: proposed the Equal Rights Amendment for the first time, 1923

Althea Gibson: first African-American tennis player to win a singles title at Wimbledon, 1967

Amelia Earhart: first woman to fly solo across the Atlantic, 1935

Anita Hill: campaigner against sexual harassment, 1991

Ann Bancroft: first woman to reach the North Pole by foot and dogsled, 1986

Ann Baumgartner: first woman to fly a jet aircraft, 1944

Anna Leah Fox: first woman to receive the Purple Heart, 1942

Anna Mae Hays and Annise Parker: first openly gay individuals to serve as mayor of one of the top ten US cities, 2008

Antonia Novello: first woman (and first Hispanic) US surgeon general, 1990

Aretha Franklin: first woman inducted into the Rock and Roll Hall of Fame, 1987

Arlene Violet: first woman elected as a state's attorney general, 1984

Barbara C. Harris: first woman consecrated as a bishop in the Episcopal Church, 1989

Barbara Walters: first female network news co-anchor, 1976

Belva Lockwood: first woman admitted to practice law before the US Supreme Court, 1872

Bertha K. Landes: first woman elected mayor in a major American city (Seattle), 1926

Betty Friedan: writer, activist, and feminist who cofounded and was elected the first president of the National Organization for Women, 1966

Betty Robbins: first female cantor (hazan) in the five-thousand-year-old history of Judaism, 1955

Carla Hayden: first female (and African-American) librarian of Congress, 2016

Carol Moseley Braun: first woman of color to be elected to the US Senate, 1992

Chase G. Woodhouse: first woman secretary in the House Democratic Caucus, 1945

Clara Barton: founded the American Red Cross, 1881

Clara Cressingham (R), Carrie C. Holly (R), and Frances Klock (R): first three women elected to a state legislature in the country, 1894

Colleen Hanabusa: first woman of color and the first Asian Pacific Islander to hold the top leadership position in a state legislative chamber, 2007

Condoleezza Rice: first African-American woman to serve as US secretary of state, 2005

Consuelo Bailey: first woman ever elected lieutenant governor of a state, and only woman in the country ever to preside over both chambers of a state legislature, 1955

Cora Belle Reynolds Anderson: first Native American woman in a state legislature, 1924

Coretta Scott King: author, activist, and civil rights leader, 1960s

Corrie Chapman Catt: president of the National American Woman Suffrage Association, 1915

Crisanta Duran: first Latina to lead either house of a state legislature, 2017

Crystal Dreda Bird Fauset: first African-American woman elected to a state legislature, 1938

Crystal Lee Sutton: union organizer and inspiration for the film *Norma Rae*, 1979 (film released)

Danica Roem: first openly transgender person to be elected and to serve in a state legislature in the US, 2017

Denise Juneau: first Native American woman elected to any statewide executive office in the US, 2008

Diane Crump: first female jockey to ride in the Kentucky Derby, 1970

Drew Gilpin Faust: first woman president of Harvard University, 2007

Edith Ellen Greenwood: first woman to receive the Soldier's Medal, 1943

Edith Wharton: first woman to win a Pulitzer Prize, 1921

Effa Manley: first woman elected to the Baseball Hall of Fame, 2006

Eileen Collins: first woman astronaut to command a space shuttle mission, 1999

Elaine Chao: first Asian American woman to serve in a presidential cabinet, 2001

Elaine Noble: first openly lesbian or gay candidate elected to a state legislature, 1974

Eleanor Roosevelt: first lady and human rights activist, 1933

Elizabeth Cady Stanton: first woman to run for the US House of Representatives, 1866

Elizabeth P. Hoisington: first woman in the US promoted to brigadier general, 1972

Ellen Church: first female flight attendant in America, 1930

Ellen DeGeneres: first openly lesbian actress to play an openly lesbian character on television, 1994

Emily Howell Warner: first woman to become an American airline captain, 1976

Emma Elizabeth Johnson: first woman president of a coeducational university, 1925

Emma J. Harvat: first woman to be elected mayor of a US municipality with a population exceeding ten thousand, 1923

Esther McGowin Blake: first woman in the US Air Force, 1948

Eugenie Anderson: first woman to be a US ambassador, 1949

Eunice Sato: first Asian American woman mayor of a major American city (Long Beach, California), 1980

Fae Adams: first female to receive regular commission as a doctor in the US Army, 1953

Fedelina Lucero Gallegos and Porfirria Hidalgo Saiz: first Latina state legislators, 1930

Florence King: first woman to win a case before the US Supreme Court, 1923

Frances Perkins: first woman to serve in a presidential cabinet, 1933

Frances Warren: first woman delegate to a Republican National Convention, 1900

Genevieve R. Cline: first woman appointed as a US federal judge, 1928

Geraldine A. Ferraro: first woman ever to run on a major party's national ticket for vice president, 1984

Geraldine Morrow: first female president of the American Dental Association, 1991

Gertrude Atherton: first woman to be president of the (American) National Academy of Literature, 1934

Gloria Steinem: feminist, journalist, and social political activist, 1960s–1970s

Hattie Wyatt Caraway: first woman elected to the US Senate, 1932

Helen Richey: first female airline pilot, 1934

Helen Zia: first Chinese American journalist and activist for Asian American and LGBTQ rights, 1980s–1990s

Hillary Rodham Clinton: first woman to be a major party's nominee for president, 2016

Ileana Ros-Lehtinen: first Hispanic woman and first Cuban American to be elected to Congress, 1989

Ilhan Omar: Somali American former refugee, one of first two Muslim women nominated for the US Congress

Isabel Benham: first female partner at any Wall Street bond house, 1964

Jane Addams: cofounder of the ACLU and first American woman to be awarded the Nobel Peace Prize, 1931

Janet Guthrie: first woman to drive in the Indy 500, 1977

Janet Reno: first woman to serve as attorney general of the United States, 1993

Janet Yellen: first chairwoman of the Federal Reserve Board, 2014

Jean Westwood: first woman to chair the Democratic National Committee, 1972

Jeane Kirkpatrick: first woman to serve as US ambassador to the United Nations, 1981

Jeannette Rankin: first woman elected to US Congress, 1916

Jeannie Marie Leavitt: US Air Force's first female fighter pilot in 1993, and the first woman to command a USAF combat fighter wing

Jerrie Mock: first woman to fly solo around the world, 1964

Jewel Prestage: first African-American woman to complete a doctorate in political science in the US, 1954

Joan Benoit: first women's Olympic marathon gold medalist, 1984

Juanita Kreps: first woman director of the New York Stock Exchange, 1972

Judy Garland: first woman to win the Golden Globe Cecil B. DeMille Award, 1962

Karen Bass: first woman of color to serve as speaker of a state house, and the first African-American woman to lead either house of a state legislature, 2008

Kate Brown: first openly bisexual governor and the first person to be openly LGBT at the time of assuming the governor's office, 2015

Katharine Graham: first American woman to be a Fortune 500 CEO, 1946

Kathryn Bigelow: first woman to win an Oscar for Best Director, 2010

Kathryn D. Sullivan: first American woman to conduct a spacewalk, 1984

Katie Wilder: first female Green Beret, 1981

Kay Orr: first woman to defeat another woman in a gubernatorial race, 1987

Kyrsten Sinema: first openly bisexual person elected to Congress, 2012

Laura Eisenhuth: first woman elected to statewide executive office in any state, 1892

Lelia Foley-Davis: first African-American woman elected mayor, 1973

Lena Springs: first woman to chair a committee at the Democratic National Convention, 1924

Lettie Pate Whitehead: first American woman to serve as a director of a major corporation, 1934

Libby Riddles: first woman to win the Iditarod, 1985

Lorna Lockwood: first woman to serve as chief justice of a state supreme court, 1963

Lottie Shackleford: first African-American woman elected mayor of one of the one hundred largest cities in the US, 1987

Lucretia Mott: cogovernor of first women's rights convention, 1848

Madeleine K. Albright: first woman US secretary of state, 1997

Mae Ella Nolan: first woman to chair a US congressional committee, 1925

Mae Jemison: first African-American female astronaut, 1992

Mahalia Jackson: singer and civil rights activist, 1950s–1960s

March Fong Eu: first Asian Pacific Islander to hold a statewide elected executive office, 1966

Margaret Chase Smith: first woman elected to the US Senate, and first woman to serve in both houses of Congress, 1948

Margaret Sanger: opened the first birth-control clinic in the US, 1916

Marguerite Newburgh: first woman to vote under the Nineteenth Amendment, 1920

Maria Frances Cabrini: first US citizen to become a saint, 1950

Maria Goeppert Mayer: first American woman to win a Nobel Prize in Physics, 1963

Marie Luhring: first woman in America to become an automotive engineer, 1920

Martha Hughes Cannon: first woman state senator in the country, 1896

Mary Davenport-Engberg: first woman to conduct a symphony orchestra, 1914

Mary E. Clarke: first woman to achieve the rank of major general in the US Army

Maura Healey: first openly gay state attorney general elected in the US, as well as the first openly gay woman to be elected to any statewide office in the country, 2014

Mazie Hirono: first Asian Pacific Islander woman–and only the second woman of color–elected to the US Senate, 2012

Michelle Obama: first African-American first lady, 2008

Mildred H. McAfee: first woman commissioned in the US Naval Reserve and the first woman to receive the Navy Distinguished Service Medal, 1942

Minnie Buckingham Harper: first African-American woman in a state legislature, 1929

Minnie Davenport Craig: first woman Speaker of the House in a state legislature, 1933

Molly Kool: North America's first registered female sea captain or shipmaster, 1930s

Mona Van Duyn: first woman named US poet laureate, 1992

Muriel "Mickey" Siebert: first woman to own a seat on the New York Stock Exchange, and the first woman to head one of its member firms, 1967

Nancy Landon Kassebaum: first woman elected to the Senate without having previously filled an unexpired congressional term, 1978, and first woman to chair a major Senate committee, 1995

Nancy Pelosi: first woman to serve as Speaker of the US House, 2007

Nancy Ruth Mace: first female cadet to graduate from the Citadel, 1972

Nellie Tayloe Ross: first woman governor, 1925

Nydia Velázquez: first Puerto Rican woman elected to Congress, 1992

Oprah Winfrey: "Queen of All Media" and the greatest African-American philanthropist in American history

Patricia Roberts Harris: first African-American woman to serve in a presidential cabinet, and the first woman to hold two different cabinet positions, 1977

Patsy Takemoto Mink: first Asian Pacific Islander woman elected to a state legislature, 1962

Pearl S. Buck: first American woman to win the Nobel Prize in Literature, 1938

Peggy Whitson: first woman to command the International Space Station, and most time in space by any NASA astronaut, 2017

Penny Harrington: first woman to lead a major-city police department, 1985

Rashida Tlaib: one of the first two Muslim American women winning a seat in the US Congress, 2019

Rosa Parks: first lady of civil rights, 1955

Rosie the Riveter: symbol of American feminism and women's economic power during World War II

Ruth Bryan Owen: first woman to hold a major diplomatic post, 1933

Sally Jean Priesand: first woman rabbi in the United States, 1972

Sally Ride: first American woman in space, 1983

Sandra Day O'Connor: first woman US Supreme Court justice, 1981

Sara Christian: first woman to compete in a major-league stock car race, 1949

Sarah Caldwell: first woman to conduct at New York's Metropolitan Opera House

Sharon Pratt Dixon: first African-American woman to serve as mayor of a major US city (Washington, DC), 1991

Shirley Chisholm: first African-American woman to serve in Congress, 1968

Soledad Chávez de Chacón: first Latina and first woman of color to hold a statewide elected executive office, 1923

Sonia Sotomayor: first Hispanic and third female member of the US Supreme Court, 2009

Susan B. Anthony: founded National American Woman Suffrage Association, and first woman on an American coin (commemorative coin, 1893)

Susana Martinez and Nikki Haley: first women of color chief executives in any states, 2011

Susanna Salter: first woman mayor in the country, 1887

Tammy Baldwin: first openly gay or lesbian person elected to the US Senate, 1998

Tenley Albright: first woman in America to win the Olympic gold medal in figure skating, 1956

Tina Kotek: first openly lesbian Speaker of a state's House of Representatives, 2013

Vanessa L. Williams: first African-American winner of the Miss America pageant, 1983

Velvalea Phillips: first National American Woman Suffrage Association woman to hold a statewide elected executive office, 1979

Vesta Roy: first woman to hold the position of president of a state senate, 1983

Victoria Woodhull: ran for president of the United States on the Equal Rights Party ticket, 1872

Wilma Mankiller: first woman to serve as chief of the Cherokee Nation, 1985

Appendix 2
Arturo Alonzo Sandoval

African-American Suffragists and Colored Women's Clubs in my quilt:

Naomi Anderson, Nannie Helen Burroughs, Verina Morton Jones, Carrie Langston, Fannie Barrier Williams, Charlotte Vandine Forten, Sojourner Truth, Ethel Williams Harkless, Elizabeth Piper Ensley, Gertrude Bustill Mossell, Coralie Franklin Cook, Frances Watkins Harper, Anna Julia Cooper, Harriet Tubman, Angelina Weld Grimké, Charlotte Forten Grimké, Mary Ann Shadd, Josephine Beall Willson Bruce, Harriet Forten Purvis, Lugenia Hope, Janie Porter Barrett, Margaret Murray Washington, Mrs. Jeffrey R. Jerome, Mary Church Terrel, Ida B. Wells, Mary McLeod Bethune, Mary Elizabeth Jackson, Josephine St. Pierre Ruffin, Mary Talbert, Sarah Parker Remond, Victoria E. Matthews, Montana Federation of Negro Women's Club, Phyllis Wheatley Women's Club in Buffalo (New York), and Negro Officers of Women's League in Newport, Rhode Island.

Selected Bibliography

BOOKS

Boylan, Anne M. *The Origins of Women's Activism: New York and Boston, 1797–1840.* Chapel Hill: University of North Carolina Press, 2002.

Crew, Danny O. *Suffragist Sheet Music: An Illustrated Catalogue of Published Music Associated with the Women's Rights and Suffrage Movement in America, 1795–1921, with Complete Lyrics.* Jefferson, NC: McFarland, 2002.

DuBois, Ellen Carol. *Woman Suffrage and Women's Rights.* New York: New York University Press, 1998.

Flexner, Eleanor, and Ellen Fitzpatrick. *Century of Struggle: The Woman's Rights Movement in the United States.* Cambridge, MA: Belknap Press of Harvard University Press, 1959. Reprinted in 1976 and 1996.

Goldsmith, Barbara. *Other Powers: The Age of Suffrage, Spiritualism and the Scandalous Victoria Woodhull.* New York: Alfred A. Knopf, 1999.

Joannou, Maroula, and June Purvis. *The Women's Suffrage Movement: New Feminist Perspectives.* Manchester, UK, and New York: Manchester University Press, 2009.

Kraditor, Aileen S. *The Ideas of the Woman Suffrage Movement, 1890–1920.* New York: Norton, 1981.

Lutz, Norma Jean. *Sojourner Truth: Abolitionist, Suffragist and Preacher.* Philadelphia: Chelsea House, 2001.

Million, Joelle. *Woman's Voice, Woman's Place: Lucy Stone and the Birth of the Woman's Rights Movement.* Westport, CT: Praeger, 2003.

Neuman, Johanna. *Gilded Suffragists: The New York Socialites Who Fought for Women's Right to Vote.* New York: New York University Press, 2017.

Stanton, Elizabeth Cady. *A Declaration of Sentiments and Resolutions.* Carlisle, MA: Applewood Books, 2007.

Stevens, Doris, and Marjorie Spruill. *Jailed for Freedom: The Story of the Militant American Suffragist Movement.* Chicago: Lakeside / R. R. Donnelley & Sons, 2008.

Tetrault, Lisa. *The Myth of Seneca Falls: Memory and the Women's Suffrage Movement, 1848–1898.* Chapel Hill: University of North Carolina Press, 2014.

Ulrich, Laurel Thatcher. *Well-Behaved Women Seldom Make History.* New York: Random House, 2008.

Wellman, Judith. *The Road to Seneca Falls.* Urbana and Chicago: University of Illinois Press, 2004.

Wheeler, Marjorie Spruill. *New Women of the New South: The Leaders of the Woman Suffrage Movement in the Southern States.* New York: Oxford University Press, 1994.

ARTICLES

Abbott, Frances M. "A Comparative View of the Woman Suffrage Movement." *North American Review* 166, no. 495 (February 1898): 142–51.

Graham, Sally Hunter. "Woodrow Wilson, Alice Paul, and the Woman Suffrage Movement." *Political Science Quarterly* 98, no. 4 (Winter 1983–84): 665–79.

Lerner, Elinor. "Jewish Involvement in the New York City Woman Suffrage Movement." *American Jewish History* 70, no. 4 (June 1981): 442–61.

McCue, Susan. "The Constitution in Ideas of the Early Suffrage Movement." *Humboldt Journal of Social Relations* 3, no. 1 (Fall–Winter 1975): 38–42.

McShane, Julianne. "Bold Steps against the Patriarchy in 19th-Century New York." *New York Times,* August 3, 2018, C12.

Robbins, Liz, and Sam Roberts. "Hunt for Relic Revives Interest in Suffragist History." *New York Times,* February 18, 2019, A15.

Staples, Brent. "How the Suffrage Movement Betrayed Black Women." *New York Times,* July 28, 2018, SR8.

Terborg-Penn, Rosalyn. "Woman Suffrage: 'First Because We Are Women and Second Because We Are Colored Women.'" In *Special Issue: Commemorating the Twentieth Anniversary of the Association of Black Women Historians 1979–1999. Negro History Bulletin* 63, no. 1–4 (2000): 63–70.

Tutt, Juliana. "'No Taxation without Representation' in the American Woman Suffrage Movement." *Stanford Law Review* 62, no. 5 (May 2010): 1473–1512.

Watkins, Valethia. "Votes for Women: Race, Gender, and W. E. B. Du Bois's Advocacy of Woman Suffrage." *Phylon* 53, no. 2 (Winter 2016): 3–19.

Index of Suffragists